SOMERSET & DORSET
LOCOMOTIVE HISTORY

SOMERSET & DORSET LOCOMOTIVE HISTORY

D. BRADLEY
and
D. MILTON

DAVID & CHARLES : NEWTON ABBOT

Set in 11pt Baskerville, 2pt leaded
and Printed in Great Britain
by Latimer Trend & Company Ltd Plymouth
for David & Charles (Holdings) Limited
South Devon House   Newton Abbot   Devon

CONTENTS

LIST OF ILLUSTRATIONS

PREFACE

To many the Somerset & Dorset was a homely railway that kindled enthusiasm. It meant a lengthy and not over-rapid journey to Bournemouth and the South through rural beauty to seaside leisure where for a time the stresses of work and home might be forgotten. Its locomotives, blue as the summer sea, performed with a willing confidence that made light of the windswept Mendips.

Although but a small railway whose independence was lost as long ago as 1875, the Somerset & Dorset in recent years has formed the subject of several books and a number of magazine articles. Undoubtedly the best of these was the scholarly work by Robin Atthill in 1967, though like its predecessors it, too, offered only the briefest of locomotive details. Space in a standard David & Charles railway history is at a premium and seldom permits more generous treatment, but it does create a demand for greater knowledge of the locomotives concerned which can only be fulfilled by a complete book on the subject. So with this in mind the present history was written to offer Somerset & Dorset motive power in its entirety from the earliest days to the closure by British Rail. To obtain this end full use was made of the minute books, registers and drawings preserved at Derby Works, Clapham Museum and the British Transport Historical Records Department, London, as well as the knowledge of the men who knew and worked the line.

CHAPTER ONE

THE BEGINNING AND ENDING OF
THE LINE

The Somerset & Dorset Railway came into being on 1 September 1862 following the amalgamation of the Somerset Central and Dorset Central companies. Of these the first mentioned was the senior partner, it having been incorporated under an Act of 17 June 1852 to construct a single-track, broad-gauge railway between Highbridge Wharf and Glastonbury, a distance of some 12¼ miles. Work commenced in April 1853 and proceeded with such rapidity that it was opened to traffic on 28 August 1854. The directors had no practical experience of managing a railway so very wisely leased the working for seven years to the Bristol & Exeter Railway who also accepted responsibility for the 1858–9 extensions to Burnham and Wells.

Unlike the Somerset Central, the Dorset Central Railway was a standard- or narrow-gauge line 10¼ miles in length which extended from Wimborne Junction on the London & South Western Railway to Blandford. It had been authorised by an Act of 29 July 1856 and officially opened on 31 October 1860. Again, responsibility for its operation was vested in an existing company, in this case the London & South Western.

Both companies had authorisation for expansion, the Somerset Central to meet the Wilts, Somerset & Weymouth Railway at Wyke Champflower and the Dorset Central to extend onwards to Cole. Obviously these extensions were intended to connect with one another and with this in mind authority was requested for amalgamation as the Somerset & Dorset Railway.

Authorisation was granted on 7 August 1862 and the united company commenced operating as such on 1 September 1862. A unified gauge throughout was gained by conversion of the broad-gauge section to standard. The extension from Glastonbury to Templecombe had opened some months earlier on 3 February 1862 and when the final link to Blandford was completed on 31 August 1863 the company, by virtue of running powers to Hamworthy (Poole, LSWR), controlled a railway stretching between the Bristol and English Channels. Engines and rolling stock had been ordered the previous year, and with their delivery the directors were able to operate their own services.

Traffic was not heavy because much of the route only served scattered rural communities while Burnham was found incapable of being transformed into a sizeable port without expending a quarter of a million pounds, a sum no small railway could expect to realise. Even so the company paid its way in so far that the receipts exceeded the working expenses and the financial position would have been tolerable if the outstanding debts had not been excessive. As it was the directors were incessantly struggling to acquire sufficient capital to pay for an adequate supply of locomotives and rolling stock and very little money, if any, could be spared for the maintenance or renewal of the permanent way and buildings which perforce had to be allowed to deteriorate.

A further traffic outlet was essential and once attempts to reach the docks at Bristol had failed the directors were forced to borrow more money and construct an extension northwards from Evercreech to Bath. When opened on 20 July 1874 this gave access to the Midland Railway and the industrial North of England as well as tapping en route the coal and mineral wealth of north Somerset. The entire future of the Somerset & Dorset was gambled on this line and for the briefest of periods the directors must have enjoyed thoughts of success for there was an immediate influx of goods and passenger traffic, but unfortunately both the rolling stock and track were inadequate while the standard of staff training was unbelievably low.

Receipts barely met the interest of the No 1 debentures so there was no question of any payments being made on the ordinary or Bath Extension shares, or for that matter on the majority of debentures where arrears of interest were steadily accumulating. Under the circumstances there was little the directors could do except allow the company's affairs to relapse into bankruptcy or to find a purchaser for the line. As the lesser of two evils the latter was chosen, but this posed the leading question: who?

The Great Western appeared the most likely candidate, but on being approached made no firm offer, which gave time for the London & South Western to combine with the Midland to make a competitive bid. This proved readily acceptable to the harassed Somerset & Dorset directors who, from 1 November 1875, leased the line to these two companies for 999 years. Under the terms the Midland took charge of the locomotives and rolling stock while the South Western accepted responsibility for the civil engineering, permanent way and the signalling. By the introduction of more powerful engines, better coaching stock, heavier track, improved signalling and well-trained officials, the Somerset & Dorset Joint Railway was in time transformed from a mediocre concern into an efficiently managed and operated line. Later much of the track was doubled and a cut-off built to give direct access to Bournemouth while many passing loops of those sections remaining single were realigned for faster running.

For some years Johnson bogie tanks worked the passenger services, but in 1891 they were replaced by 4-4-0s which in turn gave yeoman service over the steeply graded main line before giving way to larger engines of the same type. All, however, because of the Midland Railway's persistence with a small engine policy, lacked the power necessary for the avoidance of much expensive double heading and banking. Indeed, this practice not only persisted down to 1930 when the LMS absorbed the Joint Line's locomotive stock, but also for some years thereafter since it was May 1938 before the Stanier Class 5 Mixed Traffic 4-6-0s offered crews the type of motive power called for several decades earlier. The same restrictive measures applied to the goods services down to 1914 when even Derby accepted the impracticability of hauling heavy coal trains over the wind-swept Mendips with diminutive o-6-os, and belatedly supplied 2-8-os. Incidentally, like the Lickey banker, they did not foreshadow a change of Midland policy as six-coupled engines continued to be built for that company's heaviest freight services until the 1923 Grouping.

The Midland and London & South Western remained in charge of the line until 31 December 1922 when control passed to the newly created LMS and Southern Railways. As before, the former took responsibility for the locomotives and rolling stock while the latter managed the civil engineering and signalling. The Joint line's locomotive department still retained its separate identity until January 1930 when control passed to the LMS and the locomotives were incorporated in the company's stock. Ex-Midland or LMS locomotives in general worked the services until World War II when much of the motive power was supplied by the Southern so that better use could be made of the displaced engines elsewhere on the LMS. At Nationalisation the entire Somerset & Dorset section was incorporated in the Southern Region, although its operation was the responsibility of the assistant district operating superintendent of the London Midland Region located at Bath. This region also provided the locomotives and rolling stock. In January 1950 a change in regional boundaries placed the line north of Cole under Western Region administration, though its operation was vested in the Southern Region, again with stock loaned by the London Midland Region. The motive power depots at Bath, Radstock, Highbridge, Templecombe and Branksome were transferred to the Southern Region in the following month while the locomotives changed their allegiance in April 1953. Further changes on 1 February 1958 gave complete control to the Western Region north of Henstridge, and this included the locomotives stationed at Templecombe, Highbridge, Radstock and Bath. On the same date the district office at Bath was closed, although the control office remained in being as a sub-office of Bristol Control until April 1962, while finally in January 1963, with the transfer of the ex-London & South Western Salisbury–Exeter main line to the Western Region, the divisional boundary was redrawn between Shillingstone and Blandford.

Financially the Somerset & Dorset had lost money since World War I, but by stringent economy and in consideration of the flourishing summer holiday traffic from the Midlands and North no closures occurred before October 1951 when the Wells branch ceased to be operated and the passenger services between Highbridge and Burnham were withdrawn. A year later, on 1 December 1952, the Bridgwater branch was similarly curtailed while in 1958 various halts were closed. However, worse was soon to follow, for with the virtual takeover of the line by the Western Region every legal effort was attempted to divert traditional goods traffic to less direct routes, to discourage the use of the through holiday services and to urge local passengers to travel by bus. Such goods traffic as remained in 1963–5 was concentrated inconveniently at the larger stations while well-patronised stations were relegated to unstaffed halts and the passenger services subtly rescheduled to provide trains when not required and few at busy periods. The inevitable came on 7 March 1966 when all services were withdrawn except for access to sidings at Bath, Writhlington, Bason Bridge and Blandford. Even so the Co-op siding at Bath was closed in November 1967, which left the yard there to be served as a siding from Mangotsfield North Junction until December 1969 when main line services ceased to run via this junction and this branch was worked as a siding throughout from Yate South. Prior to this, in January 1969, Blandford had gone out of business, which left only the Writhlington coal traffic and the Bason Bridge milk tanker services, while even the latter ceased in December 1972.

CHAPTER TWO

THE EARLY LOCOMOTIVES, 1851 to 1874

Little has been recorded of the locomotives used by the Bristol & Exeter Railway to work the Somerset Central services during the broad-gauge period, although it can probably be assumed that most of the older classes took a turn on the line. The first train was headed by 2-2-2 tank No 33 (E. B. Wilson & Co, 1851) while 4-4-0 saddle tank No 47 (Rothwell, 1855) was so engaged on 17 May 1857, for it was derailed on that day by a faulty point in the sidings at Glastonbury. The only other engine mentioned in contemporary records was 0-6-0 No 23 (Stothert & Slaughter, 1849) which was hired at £2 2s 0d (£2.10) per day exclusive of fuel and water during the construction of the Wells extension.

Likewise the Dorset Central Railway, which opened from Wimborne to Blandford on 1 November 1860 and from Templecombe to Cole a year later, made use of a neighbouring company's motive power and rolling stock. In its case the standard-gauge London & South Western Railway obliged. The working between Wimborne and Blandford continued until the amalgamated Somerset Central and Dorset Central companies took over on 31 August 1863, but that from Templecombe to Cole ceased with the opening of the line from Glastonbury on 3 February 1862. Fortunately the South Western recorded the engines involved, those used on the Wimborne–Blandford section being No 15 *Mars* (2-2-2 well tank), No 41 *Ajax* (2-4-0) and on the Templecombe–Cole section No 145 *Hood* (2-4-0 well tank), No 53 *Mazeppa* (2-2-2), No 58 *Sultan* (2-2-2), No 61 *Snake* (2-2-2), and No 49 *Bison* (0-6-0).

Once the possibility of joining forces with the Dorset Central had been fully appreciated, the directors of the Somerset Central decided to convert their track to standard gauge at an early date and on 30 July 1861 advertised in the railway press for tenders. Prior to this, on 21 September 1860, the company's engineer, Mr Gregory, had been instructed to prepare drawings for locomotives, carriages and goods wagons in consultation with Mr Pearson of the Bristol & Exeter Railway. These, together with the estimated costs, were presented to the Board on 21 December 1860 when tenders were invited from a number of reputable builders. Those received were read over and discussed on 1 February 1861 when the lowest by George England of Hatcham Ironworks, New Cross, London, was accepted, and on the following day eight four-coupled engines at £1,850 each and six four-wheeled tenders at £300 each were ordered for delivery in August and September 1861. On 22 March 1861 Gregory reported that on his instructions one of the tenderless engines was to be modified and fitted with a water tank at an extra cost of £150. Unusually for the period construction went ahead as scheduled, so by 1 July the six tenders and four of the engines were assembled and awaiting orders as to delivery. Unfortunately, the Somerset Central was unable to accommodate them and on 29 September wrote requesting their storage under cover at their expense until the Templecombe–Highbridge line could accept standard-gauge engines. As space was unavailable at New Cross this request was refused and resort was made to the South Western's offer of free siding space in the open at Salisbury. Robert Andrews was appointed locomotive superintendent at £300 per annum on 17 August 1861 and on 9 October he was ordered to make arrangements for all eight engines to be steamed within ten days and the faults discovered notified at once to the makers for immediate rectification. Towards the end of the month one engine was transferred to Templecombe to assist with the construction of the line to Cole (Bruton) while by mid-November 1861 all were off the South Western and on 3 February 1862 took over responsibility for working the line northwards from Templecombe to Burnham including the branch to Wells. The Wimborne–Blandford section remained isolated and in charge of the South Western until 31 August 1863 when, with only a handful of engines, the Somerset & Dorset accepted full charge of a line stretching from the English Channel through Blandford, Templecombe, Glastonbury and Highbridge to Burnham on the Bristol Channel.

Numbered 1 to 8, the last mentioned being the tank, these engines were small 2-4-0s with the following dimensions:

Cylinders	15in × 18in
Leading wheels	3ft 6in
Coupled wheels	5ft 0in
Wheelbase	6ft 10in + 6ft 10in = 13ft 8in
Boiler diameter	3ft 10in
Boiler length	9ft 0in
Firebox length	4ft 10in
Heating surfaces:	*sq ft*
Tubes (186 × 1¾in)	781
Firebox	79
Total	860
Working pressure	115lb
Grate area	14½sq ft
Weight in working order	25 tons 4cwt

The boiler was flush-topped with a manhole cover on the rear ring and a pair of spring-balance safety valves over the firebox attached to a tall conical brass casing. The framing of the coupled wheels was inside, but that of the leading wheels was outside and combined with springs below the running plate. The tender ran on four wheels and had outside framing of similar construction to that currently employed by the Great Western. No 8 worked the Burnham branch, but was found to carry insufficient water, so in March 1862 a saddle tank holding 705gal was fitted. In the same month a tender was ordered for No 7 while Robert Scott was engaged for £5 to instruct crews how best to fire their engines.

The two additional engines ordered at a cost of £2,550 each in December 1862 were delivered as Nos 9 and 10 in time for the opening throughout from Wimborne to Templecombe. They were of the same general pattern as the earlier series apart from having 16in cylinders, a larger raised firebox, modified framing, a lengthened wheelbase and a commodious side-window cab. Obviously experience of Nos 1 to 7 on the long drag up Pylle bank had shown the need of greater power while the wind and rain had made the provision of cabs essential, although for some reason the tender weatherboards of these earlier engines were not repeated despite the provision of large tender sandboxes for running backwards. Payment of £2,000 was made on 5 May 1863 and the balance dispatched by cheque on 28 July 1863; the *Journal* noting—'the amount of acceptance in George England's favour for locomotives delivered, Nos 9 and 10'. The London & South Western Railway deposited them at Templecombe on 25 July 1863 and they commenced work early the following month. They were the first engines ordered by the Somerset & Dorset Railway, those coming previously having been authorised by the Somerset Central.

On 22 October 1863 they were joined by a small 2-4-0 tank having 11in × 17in outside cylinders, 3ft leading and 4ft coupled wheels, a 10ft wheelbase and a weight of 17 tons. The *Journal* recorded a draft at four months of £1,800 to G. England & Co —'for the small engine No 11'. It had been displayed at the Great Exhibition of 1862 and at the closure offered for sale to several home and foreign railways before being accepted by the Somerset & Dorset. The boiler was 3ft 8in in diameter and with the firebox had a total heating surface of 645sq ft and a grate area of 8½sq ft. The firebox was flush-topped with a dome and two spring-balance safety valves while the tall copper-capped chimney was mounted on a square base. The footplate protection consisted of an all-over bent-plate while the capacity of the side tanks at 520gal was less than appearances suggested for only the front section contained water, the rear part being just plating. This feature helped the excellent weight distribution of about 5½ tons per axle. For the Exhibition it was painted a deep blue and it was in this attractive livery that No 11 ran on the Somerset & Dorset before succumbing to the standard dark green. Later in Joint days a similar colouring was applied to engines and rolling stock.

With traffic increasing additional motive power would soon become necessary, so on 17 November 1863 a contract was signed with G. England & Co for the supply of four 2-4-0s at £2,600 each. Delivery as Nos 12 to 15 was made in September 1864, three months overdue. They were similar to the 1863 pair, but had a longer coupled wheelbase and a firebox in which the raised top was continued down the sides until waisted in at the frames. The boiler was again domeless, the large bell-mouthed structure astride the barrel being a sandbox. Unknown to the company they carried D. H. Clarke's patent smoke-consuming apparatus with the result that on 30 August 1865 a request was received for the payment forthwith of £120 royalties. This was at once referred to Englands who were later taken to court and ordered to pay £280 costs as well as outstanding royalties on seventeen engines. Appreciating that difficulties would be met over payment of these four engines, Nos 12 to 15, the directors wrote suggesting various alternative methods, and after several weeks of negotiating it was agreed that a cash payment of £1,200 should be made at once followed by quarterly sums of £1,000 until the entire £10,400 and interest had been paid.

Early in the morning of 11 January 1866 heavy snow commenced falling on the Bristol Channel coast and by midday had spread through the West Country. Before long telegraph lines were down, signals jammed and points choked with snow, but somehow the line was kept open and a skeleton service of trains offered to those unlucky members of the public having urgent reasons to travel on such a day. At Burnham the stationmaster decided to dispatch the 1pm passenger train to Poole behind engines Nos 2 and 15 after the load had been reduced to three carriages and a goods brake in which three labourers travelled with the guard to clear points and signals as required en route.

Their services must have been necessary on several occasions since it was 5.28pm when the two engines stopped at Blandford. There the 5.25pm local passenger train to Wimborne consisting of two carriages and No 13 was waiting to depart, so the stationmaster considered coupling the two trains together, but deep snow prevented the points being used; to save further loss of time the Poole train was sent off alone. The guard was instructed to inform the Wimborne stationmaster to hold the Poole–Templecombe goods until No 13 and the local train arrived, it being dispatched ten minutes behind the express. Unfortunately, the guard failed to give this vital message with the result that No 9 set off along the single track to Blandford over which the local passenger train was also travelling. In the darkness and snow there was little chance of the crews perceiving their peril, so half a mile from Wimborne Junction the inevitable head on collision occurred at about 25mph. Both engines were severely battered while all the rolling stock was damaged, but by good fortune no one was seriously hurt for the snow cushioned the fall of No 13's crew when they were flung from the footplate while the three passengers had moved to the guard's compartment for warmth and therefore were only badly shaken. No 9 was hauling the goods tender first and to escape from the driving snow the crew had evacuated the footplate for the lee of the smokebox from where a precarious and very cursory lookout was being maintained ahead. The speed was slow, probably not much greater than 10mph, and this, together with the fact that No 13's crew were slowing in anticipation of having to stop at the junction, made the impact much less than it might have been. The driver of the goods broke his collar bone when thrown clear, but his fireman escaped with a cut forehead. The Board of Trade inspector placed all blame for the occurrence on the Blandford stationmaster for dispatching the local train after the express without awaiting the arrival of the goods as instructed by the working timetable. His greatest wrath, however, was reserved for the company's locomotive superintendent when he discovered that the evening goods train to Templecombe in the winter months always included a

composite carriage to avoid the necessity of running an all
stations passenger train to cater for the odd traveller. Both
engines were repaired at Highbridge, the boiler of one having
to be sent to the works of the Avonside Engine Co, Bristol, for
attention. Despite the delivery of Nos 12 to 15, there remained
a shortage of motive power, so on 11 October 1864 Andrews
was instructed to prepare drawings for a class of mixed traffic
engines. These were presented to the directors at the end of the
year, but, because of the continuing cash shortage, no action
could be taken before August 1865 when six 2-4-0s with 5ft
coupled wheels were ordered at a cost of £2,900 each from the
Vulcan Foundry for delivery in mid-1866.

At least two passenger engines were required at once so
Andrews advertised in the railway press and on 20 October
1865 was offered a pair of 2-4-0s at £3,500 each by George
England & Co. They formed part of an order for twenty 118
class engines of Cudworth design placed with this manufacturer
at a cost of £2,400 each by the South Eastern Railway and
rejected when the delivery dates were not honoured. Altogether
fourteen were completed, of which four were accepted by the
South Eastern (Nos 215 to 218), six sold to the West Flanders
Railway and two shipped to Genoa, Italy. Just why Englands
should value the two offered the Somerset & Dorset at £1,100
more than the contract is not known, but the gamble came off
for after inspection on 29 October both were accepted without
any attempt at a reduction in price, and as Nos 17 and 18 they
commenced work in the following month. Like other Cudworth
engines they were fitted with long coal-burning fireboxes divided
longitudinally by a water-space and having steeply angled
grates. In service the two sides of the firebox were fired alter-
nately by dropping coal beneath the doors where most of the
gases were given off before the engine's movement caused the
fiery mass to descend to the front of the grate. There, all gases
passing to the tubes were fully consumed and excessive smoking
avoided. Near the tubeplate the mid-feather was cut away to
allow a combination of the gases from both compartments. It
was an ingenious system which worked reasonably well in

traffic, although maintaining the mid-feather water-tight proved an everlasting problem while more trouble was met from the complicated firebox seams exposed to heat. The framing was double, the outer set being built-up with separate hornplates and detachable tie-bars. This was also a source of weakness and one which necessitated regular inspection until Highbridge undertook strengthening at the first major repair and improved the rigidity. The tenders similarly suffered from faulty framing. The dimensions were as follows:

Cylinders	16in × 24in	
Leading wheels	4ft 6in	
Coupled wheels	6ft 0in	
Wheelbase	7ft 5in + 7ft 5in =	
	14ft 10in	
Boiler diameter	3ft 11in	
Boiler length	9ft 9in	
Firebox length	8ft 1in	
Heating surfaces:	*sq ft*	
Tubes (156 × 2in)	830	
Firebox	149	
Total	979	
Working pressure	120lb	
Grate area	26sq ft	
Weight in working order:	*tons*	*cwt*
Leading wheels	9	9
Leading coupled wheels	10	15
Trailing coupled wheels	10	6
Engine total	30	10
Tender	20	10
Engine and tender	51	0

On 5 October 1874 No 18 was involved in a fatal derailment near Evercreech Junction on the recently opened Bath Extension. At the time it was heading the 6.20am passenger train from Templecombe to Bath, consisting of a brake van and three

carriages, and was travelling at 30 to 35mph across the embankment before Pecking Mill viaduct when all the wheels suddenly left the rails. For about 50ft No 18 ran along the ballast until crashing at speed into the right-hand parapet of the viaduct. It broke through and fell to the ground below where it was followed by the tender and the brake van. Fortunately, the carriages remained upright on the track bed so no passengers were injured, but Driver Carter was killed instantly and the fireman, guard and inspector variously injured. Colonel Yolland in his report of the accident found that the embankment had slipped away leaving a dip in the line with the left-hand rails 8–10in lower than the right. As soon as the engine's leading wheels reached this depression they were derailed and pulled the coupled wheels off too. At 30 to 35mph it was impossible for the driver to stop the train quickly, which nevertheless would probably have escaped serious damage but for the presence of the viaduct. The poor standard of construction of the Bath Extension was highly criticised as was the complete lack of official guidance as to the precautionary measures necessary following heavy rain on a line recently opened to traffic. An inspection had been made at 6am on Sunday, 4 October, but despite a torrential outburst later in the day, and the fact that no trains operated on the Sabbath, no further inspection was made before the dispatch of the first train on Monday morning. This despite a severe warning, given by Colonel Rich only three months earlier, when making the Board of Trade Inspection, concerning the poor workmanship of the contractor, lack of drainage, injudicious repair of slips, and the movement of bridge piers and arches. The public opening was only permitted on the firm understanding that all bridges, viaducts, cuttings, embankments and tunnels should be carefully watched for some years. Apparently this requirement had not been passed to the permanent way foreman and therefore had never been put into operation. Colonel Yolland brought this again to the notice of the company and also suggested a speed limit of 20mph be imposed and the entire line walked over daily before the first train was run. As far as the company was concerned the only creditable mention in the report was the condition of No 18 and the rolling stock, all being found in excellent order. The former had run 169,946 miles since new in November 1865 and 1,063 since being fitted with a new crank axle, new tyres, second-hand brass tubes and new cylinders on 4 September 1874. The carriages had all recently been repaired, fitted with new springs and buffering gear in preparation for the opening of the Bath Extension and were capable of running at any speeds likely to be reached on the Somerset & Dorset.

A third engine was offered the company in October 1865 at £1,450 payable after a year without interest. Such generous terms were only obtained because the owner was George Reed, one of the directors. Although small and far from new it was gladly accepted and allotted No 16. For many years a mystery has surrounded the earlier history of this engine, but the London, Brighton & South Coast Railway's Locomotive Register offers the solution: '22 October 1865. The Old Bury engine of J. Firbank fitted with a new copper firebox, a second-hand set of brass tubes, new tyres, 14in cylinders and a spare six-wheeled tender. Dispatched by goods train to Temple-combe (LSWR).' It had been built as a 2-2-0 passenger engine in 1842 and later became LB & SCR No 4 before being converted into a 2-4-0 tank in March 1857 and sold to Firbank for contracting duties at £1,200 in August 1861. Reed must have taken possession earlier in 1865 either with his own coal mine or the Somerset & Dorset in mind. It was too small for main line use, although probably quite capable of performing many lighter tasks before being laid aside and relegated to stationary work in Highbridge Works. At the Midland valuation it was derelict and not considered as having any monetary value. No direct reference of its final disposal is made in the record books, but by means of elimination it can be assumed to be the old engine and tender sold to Moss, Isaacs for £65 in May 1876. Since no other engine is unaccountable this must have been Reed's engine which latterly was known as 'Old No 19'.

Since its formation the company had paid its way with the

traffic receipts comfortably exceeding the working expenses. Unfortunately, these profits were never large enough to cover interest payments as well as the costs of new rolling stock, so by 1866 the finances were at such a low ebb that when the debenture payments could not be met on 30 June the Court of Chancery took over control and appointed Receivers. The next few years gave little pleasure to those connected with the line for the most stringent economies were made even to the extent of refusing traffic if it could not be handled without resort to excessive overtime or wasteful working. Nevertheless the desired result was eventually achieved and in 1870 the Receivers were discharged and the Board of Directors was permitted to raise £160,000 in debentures and once again accept full responsibility of running the line.

The six 2-4-0s ordered from the Vulcan Foundry became available in mid-1866, but under the circumstances could not be paid for, and after the first two had been delivered on 14 July 1866 the chairman was forced to write to the makers proposing that they should be leased for three years at £1,000 each per annum and the others advertised for sale. On 7 August the Vulcan Foundry agreed to seek clients for the latter providing a loss of up to £150 per engine would be covered by the company, but refused to accept any alternative to the full payment for those delivered. Since better terms could not be gained the directors reluctantly consented, but it was June 1871 before the ledgers recorded the disposal of these four engines to the German government for £10,000. The loss of £1,600 was mainly borne by the makers because the Somerset & Dorset refused to repay more than the promised £150 per engine. They became Alsace-Lorraine Railway Nos 26 *Bode*, 27 *Beker*, 28 *Weichsel* and 29 *Eider* while the two accepted by the company filled Nos 19 and 20. The dimensions were as follows:

Cylinders	17in × 22in
Leading wheels	3ft 6in
Coupled wheels	5ft 0in
Wheelbase	7ft 3in + 6ft 9in = 14ft 0in

Boiler diameter	4ft 3in
Boiler length	9ft 8½in
Firebox length	4ft 10½in
Heating surfaces:	*sq ft*
Tubes (194 × 2in)	1,037
Firebox	60
Total	1,097
Working pressure	120lb
Grate area	14sq ft
Weight in working order:	*tons cwt*
Leading wheels	11 8
Driving wheels	12 18
Trailing wheels	9 4
	33 10

With the exception of carrying a dome on the centre ring of the boiler barrel they were similar to the earlier George England engines since all their principal features were repeated including the weak outside frame and springing layout of the small leading wheels, the commodious cab, raised firebox and spring-balance safety valves. When new the large cab windows could be raised and lowered in the same manner as those of the carriages. The tenders, however, ran on six wheels and held 1,575gal of water, the weight fully laden being 22¼ tons.

In November 1870 the directors called for a detailed report of the locomotive, carriage and wagon stock, and this was presented by the resident engineer, F. G. Slessor, in the absence of a fully qualified locomotive superintendent on 31 December. Complete details have not survived in the Somerset & Dorset records, but a copy found its way in later years to the London & South Western Railway and from this the following table has been prepared:

Total stock of engines (31 December 1870)	19
Total stock of tenders (31 December 1870)	18
Train mileage	593,786
Engine mileage	724,644

Coal/coke burnt per train mile	46·3lb
Expenditure on engines:	
Total	£37,138
Per mile	12·3d
Heavy overhauls in year, including new fireboxes, cylinders and tubes	Nos 1, 2, 3, 4, 14
Heavy repairs	Nos 5, 18
Light repairs	Nos 6, 7 (collision damage), 9, 10, 13, 19
Under repair	Nos 12, 15
Awaiting repair	No 17 (firebox unsatisfactory), to be inspected by a representative from Ashford Works)
Not repaired in year	No 20
Laid aside	No 8, to be made into a tender engine
	No 16, supplying steam to works
Engine sold	No 11 to Admiralty, Sheerness Dockyard, £300 (24 September 1870)

Engines Nos 1 to 10 are too small for use on the main line services especially in the winter months, and urgently require selling on best terms and replacing by six powerful six-coupled goods engines with large tenders. Should the Bath Extension be completed then four or more strong tank engines will be necessary for banking duty as well as eight larger passenger tender engines.

Having spent much of the last decade attempting to supply the line with sufficient motive power it was hardly likely that the directors would accept the report without severe misgivings. Indeed, after a stormy meeting it was agreed to ask Joseph Beattie of the London & South Western Railway to make a thorough investigation. On being approached Beattie declined the task because of illness, but offered the services of his son, W. G. Beattie, who on proving equally acceptable made a three-day tour of inspection. In general his report agreed with

Slessor's, although he was highly critical regarding the lack of modern equipment at Highbridge and the low standard of maintenance of the engines and rolling stock. He also suggested the appointment of a locomotive superintendent, a post with that of storekeeper held by Slessor since the Court of Chancery economy measures of 1867. Nevertheless it was August 1873 before B. S. Fisher of the Taff Vale Railway came to the line at a salary of £300 per annum. In the same month, with the heavily graded Bath Extension well under way, a contract was signed with John Fowler & Co for the construction of six powerful inside framed 0-6-0s at a cost of £3,190 each. All were to hand by 25 August 1874, which was just as well for the new line had opened on 20 July and the goods traffic was extremely heavy. The dimensions were as follows:

Cylinders	$17\frac{1}{2}$in × 24in	
Coupled wheels	4ft 6in	
Wheelbase	7ft 3in + 8ft 3in =	
	15ft 6in	
Boiler diameter	3ft $10\frac{1}{2}$in	
Boiler length	10ft 0in	
Firebox length	5ft 6in	
Heating surfaces:	*sq ft*	
Tubes (206 × $1\frac{3}{4}$in)	972	
Firebox	95	
Total	1,067	
Working pressure	140lb	
Grate area	16sq ft	
Weight in working order:	*tons*	*cwt*
Leading wheels	11	8
Driving wheels	12	6
Trailing wheels	8	19
Engine total	32	13
Tender (1,920gal)	24	12
Engine and tender	57	5

In appearance they were similar to a batch of Great Northern Railway goods constructed by Fowlers in 1867–8, this being particularly so of the first four which had domeless boilers as well as rounded Stirling cabs and safety valve casings. The last two differed by having a tall dome on the middle ring of the boiler, this being requested by Fisher because he feared priming when engines were working hard on the steep banks. Below the barrel there was a large inspection manhole cover, while the smokebox was 'waisted-in' at the sides over the cylinders; these also being features of Patrick Stirling's practice. On account of the heavy gradients of the Bath Extension a powerful steam brake was provided which operated large wooden shoes on all wheels. This was an early instance of such a refinement on goods engines, most main line companies making do with tender brakes notwithstanding the gradients encountered. For the same reason the main frames were exceptionally thick and robust, 1¼in, and the buffer beams were of the wooden 'sandwich' pattern capable of withstanding successfully the hardest of knocks. There were no balance weights and the first four engines also had flangeless tyres to the driving wheels. Large elliptical brass numberplates were attached to the cab sides, this being the only instance on Somerset & Dorset locomotives.

As the new 0-6-0s became Nos 19 to 24 there must have been an earlier renumbering of those engines already on the line. The exact date of this is not recorded, although it must have occurred between 23 May 1873, when the Vulcan Foundry 2-4-0 No 19 is mentioned in a report of a minor derailment at West Pennard, and 28 March 1874 when the first of the Fowler goods reached Highbridge. Probably the answer can be found in the renumbering of Reed's engine from 16 to 19. By mid-1870 it had been laid aside, but later was repaired and employed on the Bath Extension works until the line opened to traffic. Therefore it was in working order at the time of the renumberings and was relegated to the end of the list because of its age and lack of power. If the Fowlers had been to hand it would have become No 25, but as it became No 19 this must have occurred some time before their advent and yet after May 1873. The most

likely date would appear to be 30 June 1873, details being as
follows:

Original No	Second No
1 to 10	1 to 10
15	11
12 to 14	12 to 14
17, 18	17, 18
19, 20	15, 16
16	19

The gradients of the Bath Extension were so severe that it
would be necessary to employ banking engines for most trains,
therefore in February 1874 three six-coupled saddle tanks were
ordered at £2,350 each from Fox, Walker & Co of Bristol plus
part-exchange of the small and elderly 2-4-0s Nos 1, 3, 4 and 5
for which £2,550 was allowed. Thus the real cost was £3,200
each and this was the price charged for two more saddle tanks
ordered in August 1874. Delivery commenced in July 1874 and
would have proceeded at one a month if lack of money had not
delayed the arrival of the last two until February 1875. They
were numbered 1 to 5, and so four of them took the Locomotive
List places left free by the part-exchanged England 2-4-0s while
No 2 replaced the 1861 engine which was then known as 'Old
No 2'. The dimensions were as follows:

Cylinders	17½in × 24in
Coupled wheels	4ft 0in
Wheelbase	7ft 3in + 7ft 9in =
	15ft 0in
Boiler diameter	4ft 3in
Boiler length	10ft 6in
Firebox length	4ft 8in
Heating surfaces:	*sq ft*
Tubes (200 × 1⅞in)	1,055
Firebox	86
Total	1,141

Working pressure	140lb	
Grate area	14½sq ft	
Weight in working order:	*tons*	*cwt*
Leading wheels	13	17
Driving wheels	16	12
Trailing wheels	14	17
Total	45	6
Weight empty	34 tons 14cwt	
Tank capacity	1,205gal	
Bunker capacity	2 tons	

Like the Fowlers they were not only powerful but most
robustly constructed, this no doubt being the cause of their
high cost. The main frames were fitted with 'wedge' horns and
'sandwich' buffer beams, those at the rear being tucked under
the end of the bunker. The boiler was flush-topped with a tall
dome on the centre ring to which were attached a pair of spring-
balance safety valves. The saddle tank commenced at the rear
of the smokebox and extended to the back of the firebox which
was 8in into the cab, the filler cap being sited between the dome
and the spectacle plate with steps and handles provided for the
convenience of the firemen. The smokebox front slanted in
accord with the angularity of the cylinder-lines and was carried
out in the form of wings. Braking was by steam while the wheels
were dished to permit large bearing surfaces and avoid hot
boxes. Very ample sand boxes ensured that there would always
be a sufficiency of sand. Brass was used for the dome casing and
chimney cap, and more unusually to face the splashers, the
driving pair having the maker's name, works number and date
inscribed thereon. In regular service banking over the Bath–
Radstock–Shepton Mallet section they quickly gained an excellent reputation for reliability and power with the result that two
more, Nos 6 and 7, were ordered from the same manufacturer
at £3,200 each in April 1875. To pay for them it was necessary
to sell the six Fowler 0-6-0s and the first two Fox, Walker saddle
tanks to Mr C. Christian of Bristol and the England 2-4-0s Nos
6, 7 and 'Old No 2' to the Railway Rolling Stock Co of Wolver-

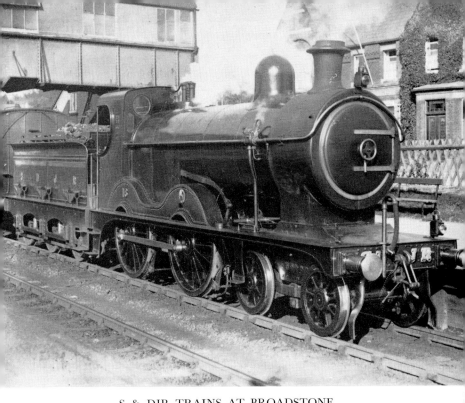

S & DJR TRAINS AT BROADSTONE

Page 33 (*Top*) Johnson Small 4-4-0 No 16, as reboilered in 1910, stands at Broadstone with a down train circa 1914. (*Bottom*) Superheated 4-4-0 No 67 with a through train from the Midlands comes off the Wimborne 'Cut-Off' and on to the LSWR at Broadstone

HIGHBRIDGE WORKS

Page 34   (*Top*) General view of Erecting Shop. (*Bottom*) The Whitaker Traverser in use. See p 195

hampton, and then enter into hire-purchase agreements which totalled £224 monthly.

Even after such drastic measures there was still insufficient money to continually provide an adequate stock of locomotives or to maintain the permanent way to main line standards. There was also serious undermanning and the quality of staff training left much to be desired. The net revenue for the half-year ending 30 June 1875 was £4,347 and of this all but £347 was necessary to meet the interest of the No 1 debentures; thus there was no question of any dividends on the ordinary shares, the Bath Extension shares which had been issued at a discount of 50 per cent or for the majority of the debentures where interest arrears were steadily accumulating. All had been gambled on the Bath Extension and success would have been achieved but for the outstanding debts. As it was there could be no assured prosperity so there was little the directors could do beyond hunting for a purchaser.

The Great Western appeared the most likely candidate, so was approached first, but no firm offer was received and this gave the London & South Western time to combine with the Midland to make a really competitive bid. This was readily accepted by the harassed Somerset & Dorset directors and on 1 November 1875 these two companies took over the working of the line. The stock of locomotives, 25 and 19 tenders, was inspected and valued by Midland Railway officials on 13 October 1875. Details follow on page 36.

B

1875 No	Original No	Maker	Date	Type	Value (£)	Notes
1	1	Fox, Walker	1874	0-6-0ST	2,350	(a)
2	2	,,	,,	,,	,,	(a)
3	3	,,	,,	,,	,,	
4	4	,,	1875	,,	,,	
5	5	,,	,,	,,	,,	
'Old No 2'	2	G. England	1861	2-4-0	850	(b)
6	6	,,	,,	,,	,,	(b)
7	7	,,	,,	,,	,,	(b)
8	8	,,	,,	2-4-0T	1,000	
9	9	,,	1863	2-4-0	1,350	
10	10	,,	,,	,,	,,	
11	15	,,	1864	,,	,,	
12	12	,,	,,	,,	1,000	
13	13	,,	,,	,,	1,350	
14	14	,,	,,	,,	,,	
15	19	Vulcan Foundry	1866	,,	1,450	
16	20	,,	,,	,,	,,	
17	17	G. England	1865	,,	1,350	
18	18	,,	,,	,,	,,	
19	19	J. Fowler	1874	0-6-0	2,500	(a)
20	20	,,	,,	,,	,,	(a)
21	21	,,	,,	,,	,,	(a)
22	22	,,	,,	,,	,,	(a)
23	23	,,	,,	,,	,,	(a)
24	24	,,	,,	,,	,,	(a)
'Old No 19'	16	Reed's Engine	—	2-4-0	—	

(a) Hired from C. Christian. (b) Hired from Railway Rolling Stock Co.

CHAPTER THREE

THE EARLY LOCOMOTIVES, 1875 to 1934

Shortly after the agreement for leasing the line was signed on 1 November 1875 Derby appointed a team of officials to conduct a thorough, yet discreet on-the-spot investigation of the Locomotive Department, maintenance facilities and the train services. Undoubtedly this became known to the Somerset & Dorset staff, but nevertheless they only proved capable of working seventeen passenger trains to time, the remaining 204 observed averaging delays of 24 minutes. Two failures on the road and three on the running sheds were also recorded. Not to be excelled, the goods services improved upon this dismal performance by not completing a single journey within the booked time. Three minor derailments also occurred, one at Radstock when the points were changed before the train was clear, and the others at Glastonbury and Wimborne during shunting operations. The blame for this unsatisfactory state of affairs was placed on the locomotive stock, which was considered unsuitable for main line passenger duties, the shortage of trained staff and the necessity of reversing all services at the southern extremity of the line. Much time was also found to be lost by the inevitable accumulative delays of working both passenger and goods services over a main line containing long stretches of single track and poorly laid out crossing points. Severe criticism was also accorded the cumbersome exchange facilities for passengers and freight at Templecombe, and justly so, since this was the most important exchange point on the Somerset & Dorset, yet the layout was such as to require the reversal of all trains using the main platforms. The transfer of wagons between the Lower

(Somerset & Dorset) and the Upper (South Western) Goods Yards was similarly fraught with difficulties.

When inspected by officials from the South Western the permanent way, bridging and signalling was found but little better. Much of the track was badly worn, poorly sleepered and inadequately ballasted while many of the points were of an out-moded design which on numerous occasions had incurred the displeasure of the Board of Trade inspectors. Of the signalling much of the equipment was modern and in good mechanical order, but was not being correctly employed, for many of the staff lacked the necessary knowledge while others had little realisation of the responsibilities entailed. It was also not un-known for lads of sixteen or seventeen to be left in charge of signal boxes at busy periods.

Between the signing of the agreement to lease the line and its confirmation by the Act of 13 July 1876 the powers entrusted to the Midland and South Western companies were strictly limited and forbade any major expenditure or changes. No material alterations could therefore be made to the Somerset & Dorset arrangements or staffing. However, once Parliamentary approval was gained various measures were introduced to improve the safety and operation of the train services, although not in time to prevent the shattering disaster at Radstock on 7 August 1876. Public attention was at once focussed on the line while the glaring deficiencies disclosed by previous investiga-tions were forcibly impressed on the joint committee whose members had not in all cases fully appreciated the liabilities bequeathed by the old company. Immediate changes and improvements were promised in all departments, although to raise the entire system to main line standards would necessarily take time.

To augment and strengthen the locomotive department a number of Midland bogie tanks, six-coupled goods and 0-6-0 tanks were loaned by Derby, some prior to the Act of July 1876, while tenders were sought for the supply of Johnson-pattern passenger and goods engines. To partly offset their cost the managing companies agreed to purchase six of the outclassed

England 2-4-0s, Nos 9, 10 and 12 to 15, for light duties on their own lines. No 9 had been renumbered 29 in August 1876 and again 29A in November 1877 while the others became Nos 10A, 11A (originally No 15), 12A, 13A and 14A in November–December 1877. Details of these transfers are as follows:

Engine Nos	Date new	Sold to	Price (£)	Date dispatched	New Nos
9, 29, 29A	8/1863	MR	1,850	7/8/1878	1399 (1399A 1883)
10, 10A	,,	,,	,,	6/8/1878	1397
15, 11, 11A	9/1864	LSWR	1,925	8/8/1878	147 *Isis*
12, 12A	,,	,,	,,	7/8/1878	148 *Colne*
13, 13A	,,	MR	1,850	,,	1398
14, 14A	,,	LSWR	1,925	8/8/1878	7 *Fowler*

The Midland withdrew No 1397 in March 1882 and No 1398 in January 1883, but No 1399 was duplicated as 1399A in 1883 and not condemned until October 1886. In the early eighties one was usually employed on the Harpenden–Hemel Hempstead branch.

Payment for their three engines was made by the South Western on 3 October 1878, and this was the date they were officially taken into stock as Nos 147 *Isis*, 148 *Colne* and 7 *Fowler*, the last mentioned belonging to the engineer's department. All were repaired by Nine Elms Works between December 1878 and the following February, and when dispatched to traffic were coupled to second-hand Joseph Beattie six-wheeled 1,950gal tenders. Nos 147 *Isis* and 148 *Colne* were sent to Dorchester, no doubt for light duties to Bournemouth, while *Fowler* was employed ballasting in the West Country. Later the former were transferred to Northam shed and rostered for the Southampton and Portsmouth services. In October 1880 No 147 *Isis* was rebuilt at Nine Elms with new 16½in cylinders, a new copper firebox, a smaller square cab without side windows, sandboxes on the running plate and a stovepipe chimney. No 7 *Fowler* was similarly treated in March 1881 and No 148 *Colne* in July 1881, the weight in working order now being 31 tons 8cwt.

Apparently few suitable light duties were available for *Isis* and *Colne* since the mileages worked were small until 1883–4 when they replaced two England long-boiler 2-4-0s belonging to the engineer's department and became No 2 *Brunel* and No 3 *Stephenson*. Both had the vacuum brake removed and a steam brake substituted while in addition *Brunel* received a smokebox spark arrester so that it could shunt the Wimbledon sleeper depot. During 1887–9 these two engines and No 7 *Fowler* were employed in the Bournemouth–Dorchester area where much of the main line was being lifted for deeper ballasting and the laying of heavier rails. Once this work was completed their services were no longer required and they were laid aside at the rear of Bournemouth shed until called to Nine Elms Works for breaking up. The dates of withdrawal and final mileages were as follows: No 2 *Brunel*: October 1889, 549,633; No 3 *Stephenson*: December 1889, 508,964; No 7 *Fowler*: June 1890, 555,903. The boilers were salvaged and gave further service in a stationary capacity until 1900–1, so the South Western must have considered their purchase money well spent.

Of the other 1861 George England 2-4-0s, Nos 1, 3, 4 and 5 were accepted by Fox, Walker & Co in part payment for the six-coupled saddle tanks supplied for banking duties on the Bath Extension. Their dispatch to Bristol was scheduled within thirty days of the arrival of the new engines at Highbridge, but payment of the outstanding costs proved difficult and it was November 1874 before Nos 1, 3 and 4 left the Somerset & Dorset and January 1875 before the last reached Fox, Walkers. No 1 was repaired at once and offered for sale, and in May 1875 was sold to the Bishop's Castle Railway where it was named *Progress* and gave useful service until laid aside worn out in 1895. No 5 was also repaired and in January 1877 sold to the same minor railway where it became *Bishop's Castle* and as the result of heavy repairs given by the Wrexham Works of the Wrexham, Mold & Connah's Quay Railway during the winter of 1893–4, when a square cab and new tyres were fitted, it was not discarded until early 1904. On 24 August 1905 *Progress* was noted partially dismantled outside the same works with parts of

Bishop's Castle lying in nearby wagons. The history of Nos 3 and 4 is more obscure after their arrival at Bristol. One is thought to have worked for a year or so on the East & West Junction Railway and then to have ended its days with T. & C. Walker, railway contractors, while the other was probably the engine advertised for sale by C. D. Phillips of Newport at £340 in March 1877.

These four engines were all disposed of before the formation of the joint committee, but the remaining 1861 England engines, Nos 2 (as 'Old No 2'), 6, 7 and 8, were all taken into stock. They were renumbered 25 to 28 in June 1876 and again 25A to 28A in August 1881. Prior to this, on 7 October 1875, No 6 at the head of the 3pm Templecombe to Glastonbury and Highbridge passenger train was derailed shortly after leaving Cole. This train was being worked tender first and consisted of three four-wheeled carriages and a six-wheeled brake van. It had left Templecombe nine minutes late, lost three more at Wincanton and finally reached Cole no less than eighteen minutes behind time. On restarting Driver Weston attempted to regain some of his losses en route by accelerating as rapidly as possible and had his train travelling at fully 30mph when the tender wheels ran over a recently relaid length of track and became derailed. No one was injured and damage was slight, this mainly being due to the guard who, noticing dust rising from the ballast, immediately applied his brake. At the inquiry the reporting officer was unable to accept that the broken spring on No 6's tender had occurred while it was being towed to Highbridge—this he considered was a minor cause of the accident; the major one being the recently renewed and improperly canted length of track. He also commented on the company's need of a weighing table, all weights having to be estimated by the Highbridge foreman. On being weighed by the London & South Western, No 6 turned the scales at 24 tons 17cwt 1qr and the tender at 14 tons 2cwt 3qr, whereas the estimated figures were 27 tons and 12½ tons respectively—a discrepancy unworthy of a main line company.

Only the lightest of duties could be entrusted to these four engines, though several years passed before they could be honourably retired or rebuilt. No 25A was laid aside in February 1882 and thereafter employed as a stationary boiler in the Highbridge Saw Mill until May 1885, when this duty was taken over by the boiler off Midland 2-4-0 No 63. It was then broken up and sundry minor parts salvaged for incorporation in the small saddle tank of the same number being assembled at Highbridge Works.

No 26A was similarly taken out of service in October 1883 and was scheduled for scrapping, but in the New Year it was reprieved and converted into a neat 2-4-0 tank with a cab having the roof upswept in a manner similar to many Irish MGWR tender and tank engines of the Martin Atock period. Little money was spent on the rebuilding since, apart from the provision of side tanks and an extension of the framing to support a diminutive coal bunker, the only modifications made consisted of new 3ft 10in leading wheels and the fitting of a hand brake operating wooden shoes on the coupled wheels. The original copper-capped chimney with its brass numerals was retained while a weatherboard was mounted on the bunker. When dispatched to traffic in May 1884 the mileage totalled 538,785, but only another 10,968 miles were run before the firebox gave out and it had to be stored pending the arrival of a replacement boiler from Derby. Being non-standard in practically every detail the wait was so lengthy that when it eventually became available in May 1888 Highbridge decided to scrap No 26A and transfer this boiler to 2-4-0 No 27A. The latter had worked the Wells branch for some years before the boiler with a mileage of 485,048 was condemned in November 1884. It had then been laid aside for some years before being dismantled, when the frames and other useful parts were stored until May 1888 when they were married to the boiler intended for No 26A to gain a neat 2-4-0 tank with the following dimensions:

Cylinders	16in × 18in
Leading wheels	3ft 6in
Coupled wheels	5ft 0in

Boiler diameter	3ft 11in
Boiler length	8ft 9in
Firebox length	4ft 10in
Heating surfaces:	*sq ft*
Tubes (170 × 1⅞in)	757
Firebox	73
Total	830
Working pressure	140lb
Grate area	13sq ft
Weight in working order	35 tons 9cwt
Tank capacity	590gal

Reconstruction was extensive, the cost being £980, for, in addition to the side tanks and a lengthening of the frames, the coupled wheelbase was increased by 6in to 7ft 4in, a square cab fitted, steam braking added and new outside framing provided for the leading wheels which removed a weakness of these England engines as built. Once again the copper-capped chimney was re-used. About 1891 the vacuum brake was added.

Apparently it was regularly rostered for the Burnham services, a report of 11 May 1887 stating: 'The Burnham line was closed to all traffic for 103 minutes on Monday last when the driving wheel moved on the axle of the branch engine, No 27A.' Later a move was made to the Bridgwater branch and because of its general usefulness for light duties a second new boiler was supplied in July 1902. Unlike the earlier one it was constructed at Highbridge from material supplied by Derby and cost £647. It had a Midland pattern dome casing on the front ring and a tall brass safety valve cover over the firebox. Also renewed were the inside frames and the cylinders. The heating surfaces were then: tubes (178 × 1¼in): 755sq ft; firebox: 81sq ft; total: 836sq ft. The weight in working order was 36 tons 4cwt. During and after World War I No 27A worked at Highbridge Wharf, the end coming with a final mileage of 1,204,647 in July 1925. Latterly it had carried a Deeley parallel-sided chimney with a capuchon.

No 28A, the tank engine of the 1861 England series, was

probably converted into a tender engine at its April 1872 heavy repair, but if so was returned to the tank status when next in works between August 1874 and July 1875, for at the Midland Railway's valuation three months later it was shown as being one of six tank engines working on the line. The mileage at this date was 298,094 and since this had only risen to 307,137 when stopped for repairs on 10 November 1881 much time cannot have been spent in steam. A new boiler was ordered from Derby and when received by Highbridge on 15 January 1883 was fitted with such dispatch that a return to traffic was made twelve days later. Apart from the use of a saddle tank and the retention of the 6ft 10in coupled wheelbase, the rebuild engine was very similar to No 27A especially at the front end where the outside framing had been renewed, although the safety valves were assimilated more to Midland practice. The brass dome cover and safety-valve casing, and the copper chimney cap, were highly burnished, while the adjustable coupling rod bearings showed the original rods were retained. In May 1891, and again in November 1901, it was shown as being stationed at Radstock, but after a second rebuilding in October 1904 as a 2-4-0 tank employment appears to have been in the Highbridge–Glastonbury area. Dimensions after these rebuildings were:

	January 1883	October 1904
Cylinders	16in × 18in	16in × 18in
Leading wheels	3ft 6in	3ft 6in
Coupled wheels	5ft 0in	5ft 0in
Wheelbase	13ft 8in	13ft 8in
Boiler diameter	3ft 11in	4ft 0in
Boiler length	8ft 9in	8ft 10in
Firebox length	4ft 10in	4ft 10in
Tubes	170 × 1⅞in	178 × 1¾in
Heating surfaces:	sq ft	sq ft
Tubes	757	755
Firebox	73	81
Total	830	836

Working pressure	140lb	140lb
Grate area	13sq ft	13sq ft
Weight in working order	37 tons 4cwt	36 tons 3cwt
Water capacity:	*gal*	*gal*
Side tanks	—	600
Saddle tank	778	—
Footplate tank	166	—
Total	944	600

At the second rebuilding the inside framing was renewed, the original set having lasted for 733,974 miles, the cab partially replaced and the bunker slightly enlarged. The boiler, like that provided for No 27A, was built at Highbridge and had a large dome with attached spring-balance safety valves on the front ring and a lock-up pattern in a Derby-style brass casing over the firebox. The side tanks were second hand while the chimney was of a built-up pattern with a neat copper cap which was retained until the last repair when a straight-sided version with a capuchon was substituted.

In the early 1920s this engine was frequently employed on odd light duties or as a replacement for failures on the various branch lines. On one occasion it was called out to Glastonbury to assist an 0-6-0 short of steam, but the lurch over the points at Cossington was so severe that on arrival the crew made a hurried inspection to find one of the leading springs was missing. It was found against the platform at Cossington. Withdrawal came with a mileage of 1,094,773 in April 1928, a figure handsomely beaten by No 27A which covered no less than 1,204,647 miles in a shorter period of time.

The only other engines of George England construction to enter joint committee stock were Nos 17 and 18, the two South Eastern Railway pattern 2-4-0s with Cudworth coal-burning fireboxes purchased in 1865. In traffic their greater power could have been most useful if the reliability had been of the same order. Unfortunately, this was not so for the complicated riveted jointing of the long fireboxes proved an everlasting source of trouble while the mid-feathers could never be kept entirely watertight. When inspected by the Midland No 18 was recently ex-Highbridge Works, but notwithstanding it failed to impress, and on instructions from Derby had the working pressure reduced to 110lb per sq in. At the time No 17 was under repair and when returned to traffic in January 1876 it was similarly modified. When repairs next became necessary towards the end of 1878 two boilers were ordered from Derby with No 18 being dispatched there for rebuilding in January 1879 and No 17 in the following April. These boilers were of Midland design and of similar dimensions to those carried by the 1878 Derby 0-6-0 tanks and the Somerset & Dorset Johnson Scottie 0-6-0s. Other changes included brake shoes to the coupled wheels, a standard Midland built-up chimney, Cartazzi leading axleboxes and strengthened tender framing. The hitherto open footplate was provided with a small cab, also of Midland pattern. No 18 was completed in March 1879 and No 17 five months later. The dimensions were then as follows:

Cylinders	16in × 24in
Leading wheels	4ft 6in
Coupled wheels	6ft 0in
Wheelbase	7ft 5in + 7ft 5in =
	14ft 10in
Boiler diameter	4ft 2in
Boiler length	10ft 0in
Firebox length	5ft 0in
Heating surfaces:	*sq ft*
Tubes (213 × 1¾in)	1,024
Firebox	91
Total	1,115
Working pressure	140lb
Grate area	15sq ft
Weight in working order:	*tons cwt*
Leading wheels	10 8
Driving wheels	12 12
Trailing wheels	10 12
Engine total	33 12

Tender	21	0
Engine and tender	54	12

In this guise they proved much better engines and gave excellent service on various secondary passenger duties until withdrawn in January 1897. No 18 on 13 September 1884 was engaged pushing twenty wagons from Highbridge to the Wharf when the driver failed to notice the signals and level crossing gates were against him. As a result the rear wagons crashed into a dray killing a boy.

In May 1891 both were relegated to the A List when the new Johnson 4-4-0s reached the line, but for some reason No 17A was returned to the Capital Stock as No 45 in November 1895. Latterly they were stationed at Wimborne from where one regularly shunted at Blandford, a particularly inappropriate task for such large-wheeled engines.

In contrast to the problems met with the 1865 England 2-4-0s, the two engines built at the Vulcan Foundry, Nos 15 and 16 (originally Nos 19 and 20), gave excellent service and were undoubtedly the best passenger engines at work on the line before the advent of the new Johnson classes. Therefore, when No 15's boiler was condemned in December 1879 it was decided to order two of suitable dimensions for it and No 16 from Derby. Delivery was tardy and it was December 1880 before No 15 was returned to traffic and June 1881 before No 16 was similarly rebuilt. All the work was undertaken at Highbridge and included new 17in cylinders, a 12in lengthened coupled wheelbase, new Highbridge-style inside and outside framing and a Midland cab. The original tenders were discarded and replaced by two old Kirtley tenders supplied by Derby to which Highbridge fitted new 1,720gal tanks of Johnson pattern. According to a report of their rebuilding made to Derby, No 15 was fitted with Allan motion and No 16 with Stephenson gear. Braking was by steam, the shoes in double-plate hangers being applied to the driving and trailing wheels, with outside pull-rods and brakeshafts behind the coupled wheels. Later, like other such rebuilds on the line, the automatic vacuum brake was fitted and it controlled the steam system which remained to operate the shoes on the coupled wheels. Despite the numerous alterations made, the chimneys retained polished copper tops. The boilers were of the same dimensions as those used in the two Cudworth rebuilds of 1879 while the weight in working order was 32 tons 16cwt.

In November 1890 No 16 ran into the buffer stops at Wimborne while shunting, but was not badly damaged although the fireman broke his arm. Both were relegated to the A List in May 1891 when the new Johnson 4-4-0s arrived from Derby. No 16A was laid aside in November 1899 and in the following month employed supplying steam to Highbridge Works while one of the stationary boilers was repaired. The latter had been installed in May 1887 and had seen previous service on MR 2-4-0 No 154. In February 1901 No 15A was similarly laid aside and used to supply steam at Templecombe for several months. Nevertheless both engines must have remained constructionally sound for two of the boilers currently being fitted to the 'Scotties' were allotted them: No 15A being ex-shops in October 1902 and No 16A in July 1903 so equipped. These boilers were of similar dimensions to those discarded, although there were changes to the heating surfaces, these now being: tubes (213 × 1¾in): 1,026sq ft; firebox: 93sq ft; total: 1,119sq ft. The weight in working order was increased to:

	tons	cwt
Leading wheels	10	16
Driving wheels	12	8
Trailing wheels	10	2
Total	33	6

The copper-capped chimneys were still carried. For the next ten years or so No 15A was stationed at Wimborne while No 16A was at first working from Templecombe but later moved to Highbridge and the Burnham services. Both were withdrawn in January 1914 with respective mileages of 979,814 and 1,073,412, the comparatively new boilers being repaired and transferred to Johnson o-6-os Nos 44 and 37.

Derby was undoubtedly poorly served by the passenger engines received from the Somerset & Dorset, but the same could hardly be said of the six Fowler goods, Nos 19 to 24, which formed the mainstay of the line's heavy freight services until the arrival of the Johnson o-6-os. They were tough, powerful and utterly reliable engines which were always well liked by the men. Highbridge, however, was not quite so pleased because the internal boiler feed water delivery piping was kinked and could not be de-scaled without resort to the facilities of the boiler shop. Their robustness was once well illustrated when Johnson o-6-o No 37 failed between Binegar and Masbury on the Bath Extension and No 21 was dispatched to the rescue. It coupled on to the Johnson's front buffer beam, put on steam, and hove the said fitting clean off.

During the early years of joint ownership they also took a turn on the passenger services and it was while so engaged on 5 May 1877 that No 22 was involved in an accident at Shapwick station. At the time it was heading the 5pm Burnham–Templecombe and was passing at about 15mph over the facing points at the western end of the Shapwick loop when part of the train left the rails and No 22 ran for some eighty yards along the ballast. The train, formed of one milk truck, four carriages and a brake van, was only partially derailed, some remaining on the correct line and others having attempted to take the up road. No injuries occurred and because of the low speed damage was slight. On investigation the facing points were found defective and of an outmoded pattern. Later seventeen similar points were discovered on the main line and on the orders of Mr Jacomb, the lswr permanent way superintendent, were replaced within three days. Strangely this engine was involved in a collision between two goods trains at Binegar on 3 February 1886 and between a goods train and a banking engine at the very same station on 5 February 1895.

No 19's boiler was condemned with a mileage of 239,764 in January 1887 and a new one built at Highbridge and fitted in

May 1888. Obviously the drawings for this boiler were prepared at Derby Works because it was similar in many details to those fitted to the 1891 Johnson 4-4-0s which became s &DJR Nos 15 to 18. It also had several features and dimensions in common with that discarded. There was a steam dome in a round-topped brass casing on the centre ring to which a pair of spring-balance safety valves were attached while the chimney and firebox top safety valve casings were of Johnson pattern. The rounded cab and the tenders with the springs within the outside framing remained, but the cylinder diameter was reduced to 17in, the pullout regulator replaced by one of Midland design, deeper sandboxes fitted, the brake rodding resited outside the wheels and double-plate brake-hangers with cast-iron shoes provided. The vacuum brake was added at the first repair for train control, steam being retained on the engine. New brass number plates lettered Somerset & Dorset Joint Railway were cast and fitted. Nos 20 to 24 were similarly reboiled in 1892-3 with boilers built at Derby. For some reason they had dome casings of the Midland 1875-8 period and not the current Johnson pattern. These five engines also differed from No 19 by having separate brass numerals affixed to the cab sides and by keeping their original sandboxes. Since the cost of these five boilers averaged £735 and that supplied to No 19 only £520, it appears that the latter must have been partly constructed of salvaged material. Dates were as follows: 1888: No 19 (May); 1892: Nos 22 (November), 23 (August); 1893: Nos 20 (February), 21 (September), 24 (November). Changed dimensions were:

Cylinders	17in × 24in
Boiler diameter	4ft 1in
Heating surfaces:	sq ft
Tubes (220 × 1¾in)	1,058
Firebox	104
Total	1,162
Working pressure	150lb (later 140lb)
Weight in working order:	tons cwt
Leading coupled wheels	11 13

Driving coupled wheels	13	5
Trailing coupled wheels	9	4
Total	34	2

Shortly after being returned to traffic with its new boiler No 23 on 14 October 1892 was running light engine through Masbury when a tyre broke on the tender. Luckily the speed was comparatively slow and the driver was able to stop before serious damage occurred. Another casualty, on 27 March 1898, had Nos 19 and 22 as the main characters. The latter was being used as shed pilot at Highbridge and was engaged in shunting seven wagons loaded with ashes when the regulator stuck open. Before Driver Miller could take any positive action the wagons were driven at about 10mph into the tender of No 19 which was waiting to be coaled. Damage was extensive to the wagons and No 19's tender was badly battered, but injuries were restricted to cuts and bruises. This was the second time the tender of No 19 had been involved in an accident for it had been crushed in the yards at Blandford on 15 June 1896 by the over-enthusiastic fly-shunting of several loaded timber wagons.

By the turn of the century the Fowler goods were largely displaced from the Bath line and henceforth did most of their work between Highbridge, Templecombe and Bournemouth. A second reboilering took place in 1908–11, four receiving second-hand but relatively new boilers from 4-4-0s Nos 15 to 18, these having closed domes and Ramsbottom safety valves over the firebox.

The dates were:

March 1908: No 19 ex-No 17 (boiler new August 1904)

November 1911: No 22 ex-No 18 (boiler new December 1904)

June 1910: No 23 ex-No 16 (boiler new April 1906)

October 1910: No 24 ex-No 15 (boiler new April 1905)

Nos 20/1, in December 1910 and February 1911 respectively, received new boilers of the same general pattern, but with a different tube layout. The changed dimensions were as follows:

	Nos 19, 22/3/4	Nos 20/1
Tubes	240 × 1⅝in	196 × 1¾in
Heating surfaces:	sq ft	sq ft
Tubes	1,072	944
Firebox	104	104
Total	1,176	1,048
Working pressure	160lb	160lb
Grate area	16sq ft	16¼sq ft
Weight in working order	35 tons 11½cwt	35 tons 14cwt

Those carrying the second-hand boilers could be readily distinguished by the location of the injector delivery clack-boxes, these being on the front ring, whereas those of Nos 20 and 21 were on the middle ring. The latter also differed by having a tube arrangement similar to the Johnson 4ft 6in 0-6-0s of the period. Other alterations included tall flowerpot chimneys, extensions to the roofs of the Great Northern cabs, the resiting of the trailing springs below the axleboxes and the fitting of 'U' links and pins in place of 'swan-neck' hangers on the driving springs. One engine, No 21, also received a new set of balanced wheels. The original tenders were badly corroded, but had to do duty until 1914 when spares became available from the withdrawn 0-6-0s Nos 27, 33/4, 43 and were fitted to Nos 21, 19, 22 and 23 respectively. Those attached to Nos 20/4 were similarly replaced from 0-6-0s Nos 36, 38 in 1922.

These engines remained in stock until 1927–8 and in their later days, having the advantage, which they had always possessed, of a larger firebox plus the higher working pressure of their replacement boilers, were classified Class 2 for freight working compared with the Class 1 of the Johnson 4ft 6in goods engines. They had, therefore, lasted fifty-five years, including a decade or so in charge of the Evercreech–Bath goods services. Thereafter most of their work had been between Templecombe and Highbridge or over the easier southern section to Bournemouth. No 19 was the first to go in June 1927 and was followed by the others in July and August 1928. Most had spent the last six months laid aside at Templecombe or Highbridge, No 21 was being broken up at Highbridge Works on 19 August 1928 while Nos 19 and 20 were nearby with their footplates stripped of brass fittings and obviously awaiting similar attention.

The only other engines received from the old company were the five Fox, Walker six-coupled saddle tanks, Nos 1 to 5, which had been designed for service as bankers on the Bath Extension. Like the Fowlers, they were new, robustly constructed and well suited to their daily tasks which they performed with the utmost gusto. Two more at £3,200 each had been ordered before the formation of the joint committee, but Johnson refused to accept them unless the price was substantially reduced. This Fox, Walkers refused and after residing in store from 15 November 1874 to 8 February 1875 they were reluctantly accepted on the understanding that an additional two saddle tanks would be supplied at £2,300 each. Numbered 6 to 9, they differed from the original series by having curved bunker tops, plain bushed coupling rods, bell-mouthed dome casings with spring-balance safety valves and countersunk riveting to the saddle tanks. Once again braking was by steam and wooden shoes to all wheels, but at the first general overhaul both series had metal brake shoes and double plate hangers fitted. The earliest existing locomotive diagrams, dated 31 December 1878, record Nos 1 to 5 as having 17½in cylinders and Nos 6 to 9 with 17in. This may have been a clerical error, although the 1896 diagram book shows the entire class with the smaller-size cylinders. They were a standard design of the makers and were supplied to a number of industrial firms in this country and abroad. No doubt various minor alterations were made to suit particular requirements. The later Peckett catalogues offered similar engines for sale from stock and used the Fox, Walker photographs as an illustration and also mentioned their arduous duties on the Somerset & Dorset Railway.

No 7 had only been in traffic for two months when it was involved in the disastrous head-on collision between Radstock and Wellow on 7 August 1876. The other engine was No 5.

There was considerable congestion on the line that day for sixteen excursions were scheduled, and Superintendent Difford, finding one of the morning down trains overloaded, arranged for a relief train to leave Wimborne at 7.10pm and follow the regular 6.10pm from Bournemouth. Caleb Percy, the Glastonbury crossing agent, dispatched notification of this and undertook to arrange crossings, although, as the driver later admitted, no less than six trains were crossed on the journey up without receiving a single written crossing order. The train reached Radstock a little after 11pm and, after an unsuccessful attempt to contact Glastonbury to ascertain the whereabouts of the down train, Stationmaster Jarrett ordered the train on to Foxcote. Here a signalbox had been opened on 24 May 1875 to serve a colliery and to break the long block section to Wellow, which in itself was a breach of the undertaking to the Board of Trade to allow only one engine in steam at a time between Radstock and Wellow. This box was not in communication with Glastonbury, so after holding the train for about five minutes at the home signal to permit a previous train to clear Wellow the man in charge showed a green light, so Driver Bishop tackled the task of getting his heavy 14-carriage train underway only to find when he looked ahead that another train was approaching at about 12mph. This, of course, was the return working of an excursion from Radstock to Bath Regatta, booked to leave Bath at 9.15pm. It was scheduled to work back from Radstock at 9.55pm, picking up en route 300 members of the Young Men's Liberal Association at Midford where a fête had been attended. Because of a rolling stock shortage, it did not leave Bath until 10.43, and at about 11.14 it left Wellow without apparently having been put on the block to Foxcote, although a few minutes later the up train was accepted on the block before the down train could possibly have reached Foxcote, let alone the crossing place at Radstock. John Hamlin, the driver, had not asked for a crossing order as he was ignorant of the existence of the up special. Running down the 1 in 198 gradient on the curve towards Foxcote, he was confronted by the home signal at danger and had reduced speed when he saw

the lights of the other train about twenty-five yards away.
When the crash came he had already got his engine into backward gear; likewise Driver Bishop had managed to close his
regulator before contact was made. The sound of the accident
was heard on the still August night over a distance of five miles,
while the continuous whistling of the engines until the steam
was exhausted added to the horror of the scene. Despite the
force of the impact both engines almost kept on the rails, and
only the down engine had its wheels off the track. The engines
were badly battered, but being of sturdy construction stood up
to their ordeal remarkably well, which was more than could be
said of the rolling stock—the first six carriages of the down train
were completely smashed. Twelve passengers as well as the
guard of the down train were killed and twenty-eight passengers
and six railway employees injured. Nos 5 and 7 arrived at
Highbridge for repairs on 12 August 1876, the costs being £685
and £743 respectively. Henceforth they were permanently
different to the rest of the class as the patching of the frames
resulted in an extension of the front overhang by 8in.

Reporting on the accident Captain Tyler laid the responsibility on many shoulders. Superintendent Difford was criticised
for the laxity of discipline and the discrepancy between the
company's regulations and practice on the line, but the ulti-
mate blame was pinned on to the Wellow stationmaster and his
telegraph clerk for omitting to exchange any signals with Foxcote regarding the dispatch of the down train.

A second accident involving the class happened on 2 March
1882 between Midsomer Norton and Chilcompton stations on
the Bath Extension when 0-4-4 tank No 32 at the head of the
five vehicle 1.35pm Bath–Bournemouth passenger train ran
into pilot engine No 8 travelling in the opposite direction.
Driver Dade left Midsomer Norton one minute late at 2.19pm
with the Bournemouth train, the starting signal having been
lowered, and when half way to Chilcompton he was horrified
to see a light engine running towards him in the cutting about
300yd away. He immediately opened the whistle and kept it so,
shut off steam, applied the brakes and reversed his engine, and

had brought the train to a halt before the light engine collided at 20–30mph. The force of impact was such that No 8's bunker was crushed against the boiler back, the saddle tank shifted along the boiler top, the frames buckled for 5ft and the steam pipe from the boiler fractured. Steam and scalding water invaded the footplate severely burning the driver and fireman, the former dying the same evening, but his partner recovered and eventually returned to duty. The crew of No 32 either jumped clear or were flung off the footplate and badly shaken, while the guard and eleven passengers reported minor injuries. The leading carriage was badly damaged as was No 32 which had its buffer beam and buffers completely smashed, the smoke-box stove in, the cylinder and valve chest covers broken, the main frames opened out and twisted, and both tanks split along the front riveting. At the inquiry it was stated that No 8 had banked the 10.40am Bath–Templecombe goods from Radstock to Masbury summit and was scheduled to cross the passenger train at Chilcompton on the journey-back light engine. It stopped at this station for water, but restarted against the signals at danger while the fireman was still on the tank top. The latter noticed the signal, but thought it had shown green and then been returned to danger during his passage to the footplate. He did not keep a look-out because of trouble with an injector and only saw the passenger-train seconds before impact, his driver apparently not seeing it at all. No reason could be found for this as the dead man had served the company faithfully for 10½ years, his record sheet making interesting reading:

Edwin Ridout (aged 29) 16 October 1871. Commenced service as an engine-cleaner. 1 May 1874 Promoted to fireman. 15 April 1878 Passed for driving. 1 March 1880 Promoted driver. Wages advanced from 6s 0d to 6s 6d a day on 24 February 1882.

A third accident occurred on 11 November 1885 at Binegar, although the saddle tank concerned, No 9, only played a minor role. At the time it was banking the 1.30am down goods from

Bath which was in charge of a Johnson 0-6-0 when the latter was run into by an up goods headed by bogie tank No 53 whose crew had passed signals at danger. Both train engines were badly damaged and many of the wagons wrecked while the fireman of the up train lost his life.

Potentially even more alarming was the near boiler explosion when No 2 was running light engine on the early morning of 14 August 1884. It had banked a permanent way special to Masbury summit and was returning to Radstock when it was held by signals at Chilcompton awaiting the arrival of a goods. A gang of men was busy replacing a number of sleepers damaged by a minor derailment the previous evening and the foreman noticed steam escaping low down from the firebox casing. He informed the driver, but at this moment the awaited goods arrived and the signals were pulled off for No 2, so Driver Reddy made a hasty inspection and, apparently finding all well, set off for Midsomer Norton. However, the warning must have puzzled him since on reaching this station he stopped by the signalbox and made a more thorough investigation to find steam was escaping from the firebox. Shouting to his fireman the two frantically flung out the fire and then tampered with the safety valves until the head of steam was rapidly reduced. The fracture in the firebox gradually widened, but no explosion occurred although the fireman scalded his left arm badly while on the saddle tank adjusting the spring balances. Later in the day No 2 was towed to Radstock and in course of time reached Highbridge for attention. On hearing of the occurrence Derby sent instructions for the boiler to be removed from the frames and dispatched for inspection by the works boilersmith. A visual check on the remaining boilers of the class was also ordered. On inquiry at Radstock it came to light that this engine had recently been lit up after washout with the boiler only partly filled with water. No serious damage could be found and 1,693 miles had since been run without the regular driver noticing any serious consequences. Derby was not impressed and immediately revised and tightened the rules regarding the inspection of locomotive boilers.

A new boiler was built at Derby and in August 1885 fitted to No 2 at Highbridge. It had the following dimensions:

Diameter	4ft 2in
Length	10ft 3½in
Firebox length	5ft 0in
Heating surfaces:	*sq ft*
Tubes (213 × 1¾in)	1,037
Firebox	84
Total	1,121
Working pressure	140lb
Grate area	14·6sq ft

Weight in working order:
12 tons 17cwt + 15 tons 0cwt + 13 tons 4cwt =
41 tons 1cwt

This boiler was of the same standard Midland pattern as fitted to the 0-6-0 shunters of the period, but with the barrel lengthened by 3½in. Therefore the firebox was longer by 4in and the barrel shorter by 2½in than the original. The dome was made tall to suit the saddle tank and was encased by the brass cover provided by Fox, Walkers. Other changes included 17in cylinders, smaller sand containers, an additional direct-loaded safety valve in a brass casing over the firebox and the moving rearwards of the spectacle plate so that the entire saddle tank came outside of the cab. There had been numerous complaints of steam drifting back along the tank tops and hovering across the cab windows and also of steam condensing in the tunnels where much of their hardest work was performed, so the cab and cylinder alterations were probably intended to combat these happenings. Apparently the original intention was to move the saddle tank forward and leave the cab front unaltered, but once the work and cost involved in making a new space in the tank for the steam dome was appreciated a simpler scheme was devised.

The remainder of the class received similar boilers at the following dates: 1888: No 1 (January); 1889: No 8 (November); 1890: Nos 4 (October), 5 (March), 7 (May); 1893: No 3 (April); 1894: No 6 (December); 1899: No 9 (July). All, except Nos 1 and 8, received the modifications mentioned for No 2. Therefore Nos 2 to 5 could be distinguished by their more rounded dome covers and snap-riveted saddle tanks for Nos 6, 7 and 9 had bell-mouthed dome casings and saddle tanks with the riveting countersunk. By the mid-1890s No 5 had been fitted with the dome cover and saddle tank left spare by the conversion of No 8 into a side tank, and so could no longer be so readily classified. The boiler from No 2 which had been dispatched to Derby after the near explosion was repaired and in January 1886 reappeared at Highbridge to be allotted to No 9 in the following month. Undoubtedly this was the reason why it did not receive a Midland pattern boiler until July 1889, some six years after the others had been reboilered.

No 1 not only received a new boiler in January 1888, but was also converted into a compact six-coupled tender engine, although apart from the removal of the saddle tank and the fitting of a vertical-fronted smokebox the other major changes were few. The boiler, however, was pitched $5\frac{1}{2}$in higher in the frames. Highbridge built the tender which followed the general design of those belonging to the Johnson goods by having the springs above the running plate, but various differences made it quite distinctive. Other deviations from Midland practice included the tall round-topped polished brass dome casing, the burnished chimney cap and the cab which, unlike Johnson engines of the period, came straight down to the running plate. Before the turn of the century a standard Midland chimney and dome casing had been fitted. The steam brake remained and the sanding arrangements were unchanged. The weight in working order was:

	tons	cwt
Leading wheels	10	17
Driving wheels	14	6
Trailing wheels	8	13
Engine total	33	16

Tender (1,900gal)	27	16
Engine and tender	61	12

The changes to No 8 in December 1889 were much more drastic for it was completely reconstructed as a neat, yet business-looking 0-6-0 side tank with 4ft 6in wheels having balance weights and of a pattern similar to those fitted to the Johnson 0-6-0s. The cab was flush-sided and partly covered the bunker space while the tanks were square-ended and held 960gal of water. The boiler was pitched 3in higher in the frames than originally and this, as in the case of 0-6-0 No 1, necessitated the cutting of a larger frame-space at the firebox sides in order to allow access thereto. Again the smokebox was vertically fronted while the chimney was of the then standard Derby built-up variety and the dome-casing of the Highbridge 1883–9 round-topped pattern. Later the last mentioned was replaced by one having Midland contours. Modifications were made to the sanding arrangements while to give improved support to the buffer beams the running plate was modified, this also applying to the front end of No 1. The vacuum brake was added for train control, but steam remained in use on the engine wheels. Some doubt exists as to the cylinders of these two rebuilds, both being shown with the larger 17½in size until 31 December 1896 when the locomotive diagrams issued in the New Year gave 17in × 24in like those engines working as saddle tanks. If correct then the larger size was kept on reconstruction and the 17in pattern only substituted when renewal became necessary. The working order weight was:

	tons	cwt
Leading wheels	12	10
Driving wheels	16	5
Trailing wheels	15	18
Total	44	13

By 1888 a number of bank duties at Radstock were being undertaken by Johnson or Fowler 0-6-0s filling in time between main line duties, so it was no longer necessary to have nine bankers. Three were needed during the winter months and five at the height of summer. Advantage was taken of this to provide an additional 0-6-0 for main line duties and a powerful side tank to work the goods and passenger services over the Bridgwater or Wells branches. Apparently No 7 was also scheduled for conversion to a tender engine, but was returned to traffic still a saddle tank when its intended shunting duties at Wimborne were found best suited to an engine unencumbered by a tender.

A curious incident occurred at Radstock on 24 January 1897. No 9 had just returned to the shed after a spell of banking and was standing unattended when it suddenly moved off chimney first. Observing this, the foreman hurried across the tracks, climbed aboard, shut the regulator fully and after coming to a stop reversed back to the position recently vacated. Alas 0-6-0 No 49 had stealthily filled the parking lot so that No 9 crashed into it bunker first. No one was injured, but henceforth the culprit displayed evidence of the escapade by having a bunker with higher side plates, no coal rails and the back plate projecting backwards for some inches. Although apparently not suffering rear end damage of a similar nature, Nos 6 and 7 also had heightened bunkers, but the others only had their coal rails backed by iron-sheeting. Around the same period the brass facings were removed from the splashers while various changes were made to the rear buffer beams which originally were tucked away below the bunkers. Slightly longer and stronger angle ironing in many cases moved them clear of the bunker back-plates.

A second reboilering occurred in 1906–11, the boilers being similar to those replaced but pressed to 160lb and having the tubes arranged in vertical rows in accordance with current Derby practice. The heating surfaces were as follows:

	sq ft
Tubes (196 × 1¾in)	959
Firebox	92
Total	1,051

Grate area   14·58sq ft
Working pressure   160lb

At the same time the saddle tanks of Nos 2 to 7 and 9 were extended to the front of the smokebox, which in the new boilers was of the usual vertical-fronted pattern and without wing plates. This increased the water capacity to 1,360gal while the working order weight became:

	tons	cwt
Leading wheels	14	5
Driving wheels	15	11
Trailing wheels	13	19
Total	43	15

Either at this visit to shops or a subsequent one new wheels were fitted to Nos 3 and 7, the former being of 4ft 2in and the latter of 4ft 3in diameter, while thicker tyres on the remainder increased their diameter to 4ft 0½in. Nevertheless the boiler centre line of all seven was quoted at 6ft 6in, that is 2½in higher than when first reboilered. For a time the copper-capped chimneys were retained, but later a plain cast pattern was substituted and the dome and safety valve casings painted over. Nos 3 and 9 were noted painted black at Highbridge in March 1915 and the others gradually assumed this livery some years before it became standard for the company's goods engines. Dates of reboilering were as follows: 1906: No 2 (September); 1909: Nos 4 (April), 7 (October); 1910: Nos 5 (February), 9 (April); 1911: Nos 3 (July), 6 (April).

In May 1908 0-6-0 No 1 was stopped awaiting a new boiler and when this was available in the following December it was reconverted to a saddle tank. Therefore, after twenty years service as a tender engine it rejoined the class and once again took its turn banking on the Bath Extension. Apart from the modified framing and rounded dome casing there was little to recall the years in between. New wheels and thicker tyres increased the wheel diameter to 4ft 3in while the weight in working order was 43 tons 17cwt. Later this engine, like Nos 2 and 6, carried Deeley smokebox doors secured by bolts and clips around the circumference. All the saddle tanks retained steam brakes only until condemned.

Having returned this engine to a saddle tank it was a reasonable assumption that if No 8 was no longer required as a six-coupled side tank then it, too, would have been converted back to a saddle tank. Highbridge did not accept such reasoning for when shops were left after reboilering in October 1908 it had been transformed into a neat 4ft 6in 0-6-0 with a 2,450gal Johnson pattern tender, tall flower-pot chimney, closed dome, Ramsbottom safety valves in a casing over the firebox, the vacuum brake and gravity sanding. The weight in working order was as follows:

	tons	cwt
Leading wheels	11	11
Driving wheels	13	9
Trailing wheels	10	12
Engine total	35	12
Tender	29	13
Engine and tender	65	5

The boiler was pitched 6ft 10½in above rail level and had a working pressure of 160lb, although later this was reduced to 140lb. Braking on both engine and tender wheels was by steam. In this final form it resembled the small Johnson goods apart from having a different wheelbase and a boiler barrel longer by 3½in. Indeed, the same light goods and branch passenger services were performed until it was laid aside unserviceable in November 1927. Withdrawal followed in May 1928 with a mileage of 704,149. Latterly a straight-sided chimney with a capuchon had been carried.

The eight saddle tanks remained on their original duties until mid-1929 when Nos 2 and 4 were placed in store and their role filled by Nos 19 and 20 of the new 3F class. Nevertheless the LMS allotted Nos 1500 to 1507 to the class when they took control of the Joint line's stock on 1 January 1930, although these two engines never carried their new numbers for withdrawal occurred in February 1930. Incidentally the LMS had to renumber ex-Midland Railway 0-4-0 saddle tanks from 1506 to 1509 to make way for the Somerset & Dorset engines. Highbridge Works undertook the renumbering of the latter and in the main completed the task relatively quickly without waiting for engines to enter shops for overhaul. The numerals appeared on the cab sidesheets and LMS along the saddle tanks below the handrailing while small figures were painted on the smokebox doors between the hinges in lieu of cast plates. Later No 1505 did receive a numberplate. Nos 1500, 1502 and 1507 were condemned in September–December 1930, but Nos 1504, 1505 and 1506 remained at work although usually restricted to light duties around Highbridge. Of these Nos 1504 and 1506 had been laid aside by April 1934 leaving No 1505 to work on alone until the autumn. Its duties during August included appearances banking from Radstock. Nevertheless No 1506 was the last to leave the line, it being noted en route to Derby on 12 June 1935.

CHAPTER FOUR

THE JOHNSON BOGIE TANKS

In a sense the take-over struggle for the Somerset & Dorset Railway was the last major skirmish in the War of the Gauges and was a decisive victory for the standard-gauge companies. For the outcome was its firm linkage at either end of its main line with the Midland and London & South Western systems. Within months of the opening of the Bath Extension the Bristol & Exeter directors had accepted defeat by announcing the intention of adding a third rail to all sections of their main line not already equipped for passage by both broad- and standard-gauge trains. Undoubtedly this was the result of heavy losses incurred by the diversion of much northern traffic, especially goods, over the Bath Extension. Indeed, such was the concern of the broad-gauge companies to present a strong and united front to the rival standard-gauge north to south route that the Great Western and the Bristol & Exeter Railways amalgamated on 1 August 1876. Nevertheless the Joint line prospered as regards traffic, although being financially incapable of embarking on the heavy expenditure necessary to raise the permanent way and its rolling stock to main-line status.

Between 1 November 1875 when the lease was signed by the Midland and London & South Western companies and its confirmation by the Act of 13 July 1876 there was little that could be undertaken to improve the line for their powers were strictly limited. No material changes could therefore be made to existing Somerset & Dorset arrangements, although it was found possible for the Midland to ease the critical motive power position by loaning Johnson 0-4-4 tanks Nos 6, 1262 and 1263,

Kirtley o-6-os Nos 351 and 353, and Johnson o-6-o tank No 1128.

The use of front-coupled bogie tanks for express work caused some surprise and immediately gave rise to complaints by the South Western's engineer's department of rough riding and damaged track. Speed restrictions of 50mph were thereupon imposed, but several serious instances of track distortion occurred in September 1876 which caused the managing committee to seek professional advice at the cost of £100 from F. W. Webb (Crewe) and P. Stirling (Doncaster). Both found the permanent way of inferior quality although safe for the passage of these engines provided speeds were moderate, and the number in service was strictly limited and the track inspected daily. Of the three bogie tanks, No 6 was found in good mechanical order, No 1262 to be running with broken bogie springs and No 1263 dangerous at speeds above 35mph. It was suggested that No 1262 should be fitted with an Adams bogie and No 1263 with stronger springing to the leading coupled wheels and a Webb bissel bogie before further speed and riding trials were held.

Quite understandably Johnson ignored this advice, although adjustments were made to the springing and bogie control. Apparently some success must have been achieved for no further complaints were heard until the morning of 26 February 1877. At 6.10am No 1262 left Wimborne with the first through passenger train of the day and experienced an uneventful journey until travelling at about 35mph between Templecombe and Wincanton the leading wheels suddenly left the rails. For 200yd they ran along the sleepers and then dragged the trailing coupled wheels off as well which caused the engine to turn over on to the upside of the track and eventually to come to rest 240yd away with its chimney buried in the ballast, the bogie wrenched off and the coupled wheels spinning in the air. All the carriages were derailed, but by good fortune they remained upright and apart from the brake van were not badly damaged. Six passengers, the guard and the fireman were injured, while Driver Moorland was killed. At the subsequent Board of Trade

GEORGE ENGLAND LOCOMOTIVES

Page 67 (*Top*) 2-4-0ST No 8 as rebuilt with larger saddle tank in 1862. This locomotive was the last of the original eight ordered by the Somerset Central Railway.
(*Middle*) 2-4-0 No 13, one of the third series of England locomotives. The large dome
is a sand container. (*Bottom*) 2-4-0 No 45, originally No 17, one of two Cudworth
South Eastern Railway locomotives as rebuilt in 1880

REBUILT LOCOMOTIVES

Page 68 (*Top*) 2-4-0T No 26A, 1884 rebuild of 2-4-0 No 26A originally No 6. Note the number on the chimney. (*Middle*) 2-4-0T No 27A as rebuilt in 1888. This locomotive was originally 2-4-0 No 7. (*Bottom*) Vulcan Foundry 2-4-0 No 15 as rebuilt in 1880. This locomotive was fitted with Allan motion and the tender was rebuilt at Highbridge from an old MR Kirtley tender and a Johnson-style tank

inquiry Captain Tyler found No 1262 in good order and blamed the lamentably low standard of the permanent way and the lack of regular inspection by skilled personnel for the accident. Apparently the track had been damaged by the passing of an earlier goods train or trains which had so weakened it that seven chairs and three sleepers failed to support the heavy bogie tank.

These engines and the Fox, Walker saddle tanks were immediately banned from working south of Evercreech until the track had been renewed and a new drainage system installed. To make this possible the South Western loaned Beattie 2-4-0s *Aeolus, Aurora, Mazeppa, Mentor, Meteor* and No 231 while the Midland made available 2-4-0s Nos 51A, 53A, 58A and 59A for varying periods down to January 1878. Every effort was made to set the permanent way to rights, including the use of two South Western ballast crews and trains, and by July 1877 no less than 91½ miles of track had been replaced or raised to the required standards at a cost of £134,588.

Notwithstanding the troubles met by his bogie tanks on the Somerset & Dorset, Johnson still considered the type was well suited to the line and on 21 December 1876 sought tenders for the supply of nine 0-4-4 tanks. The offers received were read over and considered on 18 January 1877 when that of £1,960 each by the Avonside Engine Co was accepted. It was no less than £535 below the most expensive tender, that of Sharp, Stewart & Co. Numbered 10 to 14 and 29 to 32, they were delivered in November and December 1877 painted in the green livery employed by Johnson for his Midland locomotives. Like all new Somerset & Dorset engines supplied under Derby auspices, they worked their thousand mile trial periods on the Midland before being dispatched to Highbridge.

They were smaller editions of bogie tanks built at Derby from 1875, the coupled wheelbase was similar but the bogie axles were more widely spaced like they were on later Midland engines. The boilers, too, were of similar dimensions, apart from the fireboxes which were 6in shorter at 5ft 0in than those of the Midland bogie tanks, the respective grate areas and firebox

C

heating surfaces being 15sq ft and 92sq ft as against 16sq ft and 104sq ft. The weight of the Joint engines was consequently less.

The boiler was straight-topped with a smokebox tubeplate of the then usual practice, having the firebox shell round-topped and with a vertical back, the inside firebox top being flat and horizontal with longitudinal girder-type crown-staying. In accordance with Johnson's standard practice the tubes were in horizontal rows while the barrel was constructed of three tele-scopic iron rings with the smallest in front. There was a one-piece dome on the centre ring which had the joint on top and a gun-metal cover carrying two spring-balance safety valves. There was also a direct loaded safety valve mounted on an in-spection cover over the firebox and set to blow-off at 5lb above the normal working pressure. The chimney, dome cover and safety-valve casing were of the current Johnson style, the chimney being built-up and about 6in shorter than customary on the Midland. The side tanks and bunker were lower than the Derby standard, the loss of water capacity being offset by an additional tank below the coal bunker. Despite the exposed situation of the line no cab was provided, but at an early date the two weatherboards were roofed over to give a modicum of protection.

The main frames were 1in thick, except to the rear of the fire-box where they were thickened to 1½in to permit a reduction in depth over the bogie wheels without excessive loss of strength or rigidity. However, this was only partially achieved for all Johnson's bogie tanks suffered to some degree from frame weakness just to the rear of the firebox. The bogie was of the Adams sliding type controlled by rubber side-springs and the centre fitted with a large rubber washer between the bearing surfaces. In traffic it proved trouble free and gave unusually smooth riding at the bunker end.

Like their designer's Midland engines the axlebox guides were without wedges to take up the wear between the boxes and the guide faces. Similarly the wrought-iron wheels were fitted with solid forged crescent-shaped balance weights. Braking was by steam, the blocks to the front of the coupled wheels being of cast-iron with double-plate hangers and pull-rods outside the wheels. The bogie wheels were also braked by steam, but when the automatic vacuum brake was added for use with the carriage stock this refinement was discarded. For forward running sand-boxes were provided under the running plate ahead of the leading wheels and for bunker first working behind the driving wheels below the tanks. Sanding was by gravity.

The dimensions were as follows:

Cylinders	17in × 24in
Coupled wheels	5ft 3in
Bogie wheels	3ft 0in
Wheelbase	8ft 0in + 8ft 6in + 5ft 6in = 22ft 0in
Boiler diameter	4ft 2in
Boiler length	10ft 6in
Firebox length	5ft 0in
Height of boiler centre	6ft 10$\frac{3}{8}$in
Heating surfaces:	*sq ft*
Tubes (219 × 1$\frac{3}{4}$in)	1,103
Firebox	92
Total	1,195

Grate area	15sq ft	
Working pressure	140lb	
Weight in working order:	*tons*	*cwt*
Leading coupled wheels	13	13
Trailing coupled wheels	14	11
Bogie	15	7
Total	43	11

Weight empty	37 tons 4cwt
Bunker capacity	1$\frac{1}{2}$ tons
Tank capacity	876gal

The improved springing arrangements, longer bogie wheel-base and reduced weight of these engines made them much steadier at speed than their Midland counterparts and their introduction led to no complaints by the South Western's engineers' department. In part this was no doubt due to the improved permanent way. Their arrival on the line made it possible for all the remaining South Western and Midland engines to be returned home for they at once accepted responsibility for the whole of the main line passenger traffic, including the expresses, from Bath to Wimborne, and later to Bournemouth. From December 1877 the old 2-4-0s were relegated to the secondary services between Highbridge, Evercreech and Templecombe with very occasional forays to Wimborne or Bournemouth. At first the best trains were lightly loaded and so easily timed that speeds of 35 to 40mph were seldom exceeded even on the down grades, but in 1880 there was a general tightening of schedules while in the summer months the Midland commenced running through carriages from Bradford and Newcastle to Bournemouth. There was one express in each direction from the North and another train each way which included through carriages to and from Birmingham. The down train from Birmingham left Bath at 2.30pm and with intermediate stops at Shepton Mallet and Blandford, and a reversal at Templecombe, reached Wimborne at 4.33pm. The 6.20pm from Bath which formed the through train from Bradford and Newcastle was timed similarly. The distance of 64 miles was covered at $31\frac{1}{4}$mph, including stops and reversal, which was excellent considering the line remained single throughout and was steeply graded. Undoubtedly such duties were very hard for the bogie tanks, this being indicated by the fuel returns of 30 June 1881 which gave an average coal consumption of 41·3lb per mile. The yearly mileages were also high for tank engines, No 29 for instance averaging 31,089 for its first six years of service.

Performing so many passenger duties it is not surprising that the class was involved in a number of accidents, the first of interest occurring on 12 December 1881 when No 14 with the 12.18pm Bath–Bournemouth express left the rails on the Wimborne curve about a mile from the junction. The departure from Bath had been five minutes late, because the connecting Midland Railway train arrived eleven minutes behind schedule, and after stopping at various stations en route it was approaching Wimborne Junction at about 25mph when the leading brake van broke away and fell on its side, and the next four carriages left the rails and ran along the ballast. Fortunately, the latter remained upright so no passengers were injured, but the guard struck his head heavily and was unconscious for six days. On inspecting the scene of the accident two rails were found only partially secured, a gang of platelayers having removed the fish plates and the spikes from six chairs and failed to warn the driver by means of flags to reduce his speed to a walking pace.

Of more consequence was the head-on collision on 2 March 1882 between No 32 and the five-vehicle 1.35pm Bath–Bournemouth train and the Fox, Walker saddle tank No 8. The passenger train was running under clear signals after stopping at Midsomer Norton and was scheduled to pass the returning banking engine at Chilcompton, but for some reason the latter's driver set off against the signals and thereafter kept such a poor look-out that he failed to see No 32 or hear the prolonged warning whistle. Damage was severe with eleven passengers and three railway men being injured, and the driver of No 8 killed.

The success of these nine bogie tanks was such that when more passenger engines became necessary in 1883 Fisher, the resident locomotive superintendent, had no hesitation in requesting another four. Johnson agreed and sought tenders immediately, and when these were opened on 4 April 1883 that by the Vulcan Foundry of £2,295 each was accepted. Delivery was promised before the New Year, but this proved wildly optimistic for it was 9 January 1885 before the last reached Highbridge. Numbered 52 to 55, they were the only engines delivered new in the Midland red livery before the change to blue in March 1886, the recently constructed Vulcan 0-6-0s Nos 46 to 51 having been painted in the Midland green livery used since the formation of the joint committee. It took Derby from September 1881 until October 1883 to decide on the change from green to red, which incidentally was referred to as oxide of iron, but Highbridge considered the use of blue for the first time on 8 March 1886 and reached a decision the same day.

The first new engines to have this livery were 0-6-0s Nos 56 to 61 of 1890.

Nos 52 to 55 differed from the original series by having genuine Midland Railway pattern cabs, slightly higher bunkers and side tanks extending further forward as well as being heightened to accord with the bunkers. Although the chimney was of the short built-up type used on the Avonsides, both the dome and safety valve casings, like the Vulcan goods of 1884, were of the lower pattern adopted by Derby in 1879–80 while the smokebox front handrailing had the simple sweep round from the sides used by Derby since 1875. Cab doors were provided, this not only being an innovation on the Somerset & Dorset, but also on the Midland where it was 1889 before such refinements appeared on the 0-4-4 tanks. Braking was by steam, that on the bogie being removed when the vacuum system was added in the early 1890s. The boiler and most of the dimensions were similar to those of the earlier series, but the water capacity was increased to 950gal and the working order weight slightly less at 43 tons 7cwt (12 tons 18cwt + 14 tons 18cwt + 15 tons 11cwt). Reversing was by means of the standard Johnson bogie tank layout of a screw and double-handed arm in which the screw operated a lever pivoted at its centre to the side of the tank. This caused the screw-block to be towards the rear of the engine when in forward and vice versa when in backward gear, which on occasions after dark could cause confusion to the inexperienced. Indeed, this proved so on 27 February 1885 when No 53 was only a few weeks old. At the time it was shunting loaded stone wagons at Shepton Mallet in charge of a young fireman, the driver having walked over to speak to the signalman, when the former accidentally moved off in the wrong direction and pushed five wagons through the buffers before he could stop. No one was injured, but rerailing was difficult and took all night with subsequent delays to other traffic.

A few months later, on Friday, 13 July 1885, the same engine was involved in another incident when heading the 11.45am Bournemouth–Bath passenger train through Binegar station.

Earlier in the morning Colonel Rich had been in attendance on behalf of the Board of Trade when the new second track had been opened to traffic between Binegar and Chilcompton. Previously he had found fault in the signalbox locking-bars and had suggested improvements, but these had not been completed before the opening and a fitter was ordered to attend to them forthwith. Therefore with the knowledge of all concerned one locking-bar was removed for modification and the signalman left to operate his box without safeguards. All was well until 2.06pm when 0-6-0 No 48 on a down goods train from Bath, consisting of twenty-five wagons, two brake vans and banking engine No 5, was standing on the down line in Binegar station. The signals were off for No 53 and its train to pass through without stopping, but by error the signalman had set the points incorrectly and instead of taking its appointed path this train ran along the down line and crashed into the stationary goods at 20 to 25mph. If the locking-bar had been in place then the accident could not have happened because the signals could not have been pulled off until the points had been set correctly. One passenger was killed instantly, the passenger guard died soon after, the driver and fireman of No 53 were severely injured and fourteen passengers rather less so. As the two engines met head on both had broken buffer beams, bent frames, shifted cylinders and motion, smashed smokeboxes and buckled running plates. Of the rolling stock the leading passenger van was wrecked and the 3rd class carriage next to it smashed all but for one compartment while the framing of the next composite was driven 16ft under the following carriage. The tender of No 48 was lifted by the impact on to the leading wagons, smashing two of them completely. The inspecting officer considered that the accident could have been avoided, despite the signalman's error, if continuous brakes had been fitted to the passenger train. No 53 had the steam brake on all eight wheels while the carriages were equipped with chain brakes, the leading van and three carriages being controlled by the driver and the rear van by the guard. As the speed was still 20 to 25mph on impact after a 160ft warning, undoubtedly this was correct.

Like ships some engines are thought lucky and others the very reverse. No 53 was obviously a fully paid up member of the last-mentioned club because on 3 February 1886 it was again in trouble at Binegar. On this occasion it had left Shepton Mallet at 2.30am with eight loaded wagons, twenty-five empties and two brake vans; assistance at the rear being given by Scottie No 39. The train was approaching Binegar in moderate to dense fog when the signals were found to be at danger. This in itself was not particularly dangerous, but the signalman had lowered the signals for the down 1.30am Bath–Bournemouth goods headed by o-6-o No 36 and banked by o-6-o saddle tank No 9. This train passed through Binegar station at about 15mph and without stopping entered the single-track section to Masbury where it crashed head on with No 53 which was still moving at around 7mph. Damage was extensive with wrecked wagons scattered over some hundred yards of track, but only No 53's fireman was killed, the other employees being variously injured. At the inquiry blame was shared by Signalman Cox for lowering his down signals before the up train had entered the loop and No 36's driver for breaking Rule 359. This stated that under no circumstances must a driver start from a station when another train is appointed to meet and pass at that station before such train has arrived. It was recommended that the train staff or tablet system should be introduced at once on all single-line sections of the railway. At the coroner's court Signalman Cox was found guilty of manslaughter.

The next report of No 53 is found on 1 January 1887 when Driver Wilkinson was fined £2 for losing time with a Bath–Templecombe excursion. His defence rested on his engine being unsafe for high speed on account of flats on the coupled wheels. On inspection No 53 was not found to suffer from this impediment, but three other bogie tanks were found to do so and instructions were given that the class must only be used for goods work when no other engines were available.

No 54, of the same series, also came to grief on 23 December 1890 when entering Broadstone Junction station 70 minutes late with the 2.15pm Bath–Bournemouth West passenger train composed of seven carriages and a brake van. Between the signalbox and the platform it came into violent collision with the tender of LSWR 0-6-0 No 290 which was being worked light engine from Wimborne to Bournemouth and had been stationary for several minutes awaiting signals. Suddenly its driver moved off without authority and was immediately halted again by a shout from the signalbox where the signalman hastily pulled all signals to danger, but he was too late for the Somerset & Dorset train was almost on the light engine whose driver only had time to open wide his regulator before contact was made. This was so destructive that No 290's tender was crushed for half its length and the trailing wheels wrenched off while the engine was thrust forward some 280yd. No 54 left the rails and after running 55yd with the tender wheels beneath it came to rest slewed across both tracks of the Poole–Bournemouth line. The frames were opened up, footplating buckled, smokebox front battered in, the boiler moved 11in backwards, the right-hand tank punctured, and all the brake, sanding and buffering gear wrecked. The leading van was telescoped into the first carriages and the other vehicles variously damaged, but the casualties were remarkably few, one passenger being killed and three badly injured while No 54's crew was severely shaken. The guard in the leading van had a miraculous escape for not only was his van telescoped and torn apart but he was flung into the path of the following vehicles to emerge from the debris with a cut hand and sundry bruises. At the inquiry the South Western crew were blamed for the occurrence, although it was considered that the accident would have been avoided if their engine's tail lamp had been lighted. The real cause, however, was probably fatigue, for both men had worked excessively long hours, having shunted at Bournemouth East from 6.25am to 10.55am and then run light engine to Branksome Junction for another spell of shunting before proceeding to Wimborne. There more shunting, interspersed with working passenger trains to Bournemouth West and back, was undertaken until 5.10pm when the journey light engine to Bournemouth East was commenced. So both men had been some eleven hours on duty with only five hours at home since working 14¾ hours the previous day.

The Avonside batch were supplied with new boilers in 1889–94. These were similar to those discarded, except that 246 × 1⅝in tubes were fitted giving heating surfaces of tubes 1,151sq ft, firebox 100sq ft, total 1,251sq ft. The working pressure was again 140lb, but the grate area at 14¾sq ft was slightly smaller. Some engines, such as Nos 10, 14 and 30, received new 18in × 24in cylinders, although many kept the smaller size until after the turn of the century. Dates of reboilering were: 1889: No 29 (November); 1890: No 12 (March); 1891: Nos 10 (January), 14 (July), 31 (April); 1892: No 11 (February); 1893: Nos 30 (August), 32 (December); 1894: No 13 (October). At the same time new cabs of standard pattern but shorter than those on the Vulcans were fitted and coal rails added to the bunker tops, while in February 1897 No 14 was relegated to the A list to make way for one of the new Johnson 4-4-0s built at Derby. By this period few main-line services were being worked, these mainly being the province of the more powerful 4-4-0s, and henceforth the bogie tanks spent much of their time on local or branch duties. They were mostly stationed at Highbridge and Templecombe, though Bridgwater and Wells usually had one apiece. Nos 52 to 55 were similarly given new Johnson boilers in the early 1900s. The replacements were of steel in two rings with the dome on the front one, but otherwise had the same tube layout, heating surfaces and grate area as those provided for the Avonside series. All had previously been equipped with bunker coal rails. Dates of reboilering were: No 52: September 1902; No 53: March 1905; No 54: June 1907; No 55: August 1906. Later No 55 was fitted with a Fowler chimney of the pattern used by the Midland Railway's small-boilered 0-6-0s and which had a capuchon.

No 52 was involved in two incidents during 1914, the first being on Easter Monday when it was working a crowded excursion bunker first over the points at the entrance to the excursion platform at Burnham. Fortunately, no one was seriously hurt for though the coaches and engine were derailed, they remained upright. A few months later, on 21 September 1914, it was in charge of a short goods approaching Bruton Road Crossing where a gang of platelayers were weeding the lines. All moved clear of the running line except one man who stood on the up line and was hit by an up express hauled by 4-4-0 No 77 and thrown down the embankment. Once again fortune favoured the company for the platelayer escaped with a shaking and bruising.

Between 1906 and 1910 the nine Avonsides were again re-boilered, on this occasion with a pattern similar to the 1901–3 Johnson variety fitted to Nos 52 to 55, but having this engineer's final type of mountings including a closed dome and Rams-bottom safety valves and a lock-up valve contained in a large casing over the firebox. The tube layout consisted of 196 having a diameter of $1\frac{3}{4}$in and giving a heating surface of 977sq ft, to which the firebox added a further 97sq ft. The grate area was 14·6sq ft and the working pressure 160lb. The chimney was an elongated version of the Johnson pattern applied to many Midland large-boilered goods and Belpaire 4-4-0s from 1903 onwards. At Highbridge it was usually known as the Derby flowerpot and, like the boilers, was often assigned to Deeley despite his succession on the Midland not having occurred until January 1904. Dates of reboilering were: 1906: Nos 13 (October), 30 (September); 1907: Nos 10 (March), 12 (January), 14A (December), 29 (April), 32 (February); 1909: No 11 (October); 1910: No 31 (October).

On 7 February 1906 the managing committee gave serious consideration to means of reducing the operating costs of the Bridgwater and Wells branches, both of which carried few passengers for much of the year. The introduction of motor-trains was suggested, but no decision taken on hearing from Whitaker that the South Western was offering the loan of a steam railcar for a series of trials on various branch services. The offer was accepted and on 27 April 1906 H12 Class No 1 arrived at Highbridge with a South Western inspector in charge to demonstrate the driving techniques. The following morning it was set to work on the Bridgwater services, but much difficulty was encountered keeping time with a capacity load. Raising sufficient steam was the problem because should the fire-door be opened to feed in coal the steam pressure immediately fell, yet if no firing was attempted the pressure similarly fell away as the fuel was consumed. After some experimentation it was found possible to keep time if the firebox was crammed to capacity at stations and no further firing attempted until the next stop. Even so the arrival at the next port of call was often in the hands of Providence. Brief trials were also held on the Wells and Burnham services, but with no greater success. Forty passengers and a very limited weight of luggage could be carried, which covered the requirements of quiet periods but at other times intending passengers had to be left behind. The South Western inspector hopefully suggested attaching a six-wheeled carriage and when this proved beyond No 1's haulage power it was returned home with a suitable letter of thanks.

In October 1906 fresh trials were held on the Highbridge–Burnham services with 0-4-2 saddle tank No 25A and a bogie carriage, both having been equipped for motor-train operation. Once again no success was achieved and this engine was returned to its Radstock shunting duties, leaving conventional trains to work the various branch lines until August 1927. Then No 55 and a composite bogie carriage were suitably modified at a cost of £280 and set to work on the Burnham line. Since the well-proven LMS vacuum system of motor-train control was employed no serious difficulties were encountered and in May 1928 Nos 30A, 31A, 32 and 54 with extra coaches were similarly equipped for use on the Wells branch and from Templecombe to Bournemouth. The latter proved very unpopular with the regular passengers and were withdrawn after a few months, but the Burnham, Bridgwater and Wells branches were so operated for many years.

Withdrawal commenced on 3 November 1920 with No 54 of the Vulcan series which had been stopped since the previous September with frame damage, the mileage being 791,641. Derby was asked for a replacement and at £3,000 offered No 1305 which had commenced work on the Midland as No 1651 in April 1884, new boilers having been supplied in March 1902 and July 1918. On being accepted it was overhauled and as No 54 delivered to the Joint line still painted red although lettered SDJR. Payment was made on 7 July 1921, but the transfer had occurred during the previous January. It carried more water than the Joint engines (1,150gal), had a larger firebox, 150lb working pressure and a weight of 51 tons 9cwt in working order; thus it was a worthy substitute despite having a mileage of 874,217. In April 1926 Nos 29 to 31 were relegated to the A List while No 32 was renumbered 52 in August 1928, and thereby filled the number left vacant by the Vulcan-built 0-4-4 tank which had been condemned the previous 2 May.

Prior to this three of the class had quite unexpectedly been reboilered yet again, these being Nos 32 (to No 52 1928), 53 and 55 in March 1925, January 1926 and June 1925 respectively. These G5½ boilers were a Belpaire version of the round-topped firebox variety discarded and thus had the 10ft 6$\frac{1}{16}$in barrel of the Midland G6 boilers married to the 4ft 11$\frac{15}{16}$in firebox of the G5s. The heating surfaces were: Tubes (196 × 1$\frac{3}{4}$in), 977$\frac{1}{2}$sq ft; Firebox, 96sq ft; Total, 1,073$\frac{1}{2}$sq ft. Working pressure, 160lb; Grate area, 14$\frac{1}{2}$sq ft. The weight in working order was:

	tons	cwt
Leading wheels	14	18
Driving wheels	16	12
Bogie	18	1
Total	49	11

The cabs were widened flush with the side tanks while the new front plates had four look-out windows as fitted to many Midland Belpaire engines, although the Midland's own 0-4-4 tanks with similar fireboxes only had two windows. No change was made to the rear weatherboard windows. Tall parallel-sided Deeley chimneys were used as they were on others of the class retaining round fireboxes, but, whereas on the Midland bogie tanks these chimneys had plain chimney tops, those on the Joint line had capuchons. (Presumably because more of the running was expected to be chimney foremost.) Deeley pattern smokebox doors, secured by bolts and clips round the edge, also appeared latterly on Nos 12, 30A, 52 and 55.

On 2 May 1929 a report on the Joint line's locomotive stock was issued in which Vulcan No 52 was listed for replacement at once and all the other bogie tanks on expiration of their boiler life. All were shown as 'engine and boiler non-standard', which was correct as far as the true Somerset & Dorset bogie tanks were concerned, but not in the case of No 54 (ex-Midland No 1305). Nevertheless only No 52 was withdrawn before the LMS take-over on 1 January 1930 when Nos 10/1/2/3, 14A, 29A, 30A, 31A, 52 (ex-No 32), 53/4/5 were allotted Nos 1200 to 1207, 1230/1, 1305 and 1232 respectively. To allow for this it was necessary for Kirtley 0-4-4 tanks Nos 1201 and 1203 to be altered to 1212 and 1213. However, as Nos 10 and 14A had been laid aside in October 1929 they never carried the new numbers and were condemned early in the New Year, while only No 1230 received the standard LMS black livery, the others having the new owner's initials and numerals superimposed on the blue. As expected, withdrawal was rapid, with all going in 1930–2, except No 1230 with its Belpaire G5½ boiler, the replacements being ex-Midland bogie tanks. No 1230 led a truly charmed life on a line not renowned for the retention of small and non-standard classes. First it was transferred to Wellingborough for the Higham Ferrers motor services and later worked from Skipton and Bedford before finally being withdrawn from Nottingham in June 1946 with a mileage of no less than 1,643,238.

CHAPTER FIVE

THE SMALL 4-4-0s

The regular use of front-coupled tender or tank engines for express service was frowned upon by most locomotive superintendents and civil engineers. A notable exception, of course, was William Stroudley who successfully employed his 6ft 6in Richmond and Gladstone classes on the best Brighton expresses and his D-Tanks on the semi-fast passenger services for many years. Stroudley reasoned that as the greatest weight of a steam locomotive was at the front then the coupled wheels were best sited there. This shortened the wheelbase and avoided the use of heavy castings below the footplate, yet did not impair the stability or riding qualities for the lightly laden trailing wheels forced the leading flanges up to the outside of curves which enabled the leading wheels to pass round without shock or oscillation. The reasoning was sound and certainly the Brighton suffered no derailments that could be attributed to the design of its locomotives. Nevertheless, flange wear of the leading tyres was exceptionally heavy and necessitated frequent returning, although to some degree Stroudley overcame this disadvantage on his Gladstones by fitting tyres of very high tensile strength. The behaviour in traffic of the Somerset & Dorset bogie tanks was similar to the Brighton engines, but their tyres were of a much lower tensile strength and therefore they were particularly prone to rapid flange wear. Any increase in size or weight of the class would undoubtedly have intensified the tendency as well as affecting the stability. So when Whitaker requested four more passenger engines in December 1889 he expressed doubts as to the wisdom of perpetuating the 0-4-4 tank design. Johnson agreed and recommended ordering 4-4-os at £1,950 each from Derby with delivery promised before mid-1890. Unfortunately, production delays badly hindered their assembly and it was May 1891 before they reached Highbridge.

Numbered 15 to 18 they were essentially smaller versions of contemporary Midland 4-4-os. The boiler was formed of the Derby Class A barrel and the Class C firebox while the bogie was of the usual Johnson pattern with Adams sliding pivot centre and robust bronze pivot-plate controlled by horizontal helical springs on either side. Similarly the main framing followed current Midland practice by being constructed in two sections lap-jointed at the motion-plate with the leading length inside to give some lateral movement for the bogie and yet offering the maximum distance between the frames at the fire-box sides where it was most necessary.

The motion, valve gear and rods, etc, only differed from earlier Joint engines by having a slightly modified disposition, the motion-plate remained of plate construction, but the inside cranks were hooped and had security bolts through the pin centres. The connecting rods were 5ft 10¼in between centres and the throw of the coupling rods 1ft 10in. The reversing gear was of the screw type which operated direct and not with the position reversed as it was in the bogie tanks. The driving and trailing coupled wheels had plate springing, these being hung below the axle boxes by solid hangers. The layout of the braking gear also followed Derby practice insomuch that the shoes to the front of the coupled wheels were supported by single-plate hangers with the pull-rods sited centrally down the engine. The brake shaft was exceptionally short and was attached to plates hung from the drag-casting to which the steam brake cylinder was also attached. The engine and tender steam braking was controlled by vacuum ejectors which operated the coaching stock brakes. Steam was employed for sanding, there being the usual pair of Johnson-style sandboxes below the running plate for forward working and no provision for running tender first. To prevent the spilling of sand over the slide bars and motion when topping up the boxes small angle-strips were riveted along the inner edge of the running plate between the smokebox and the motion plate. This was a feature peculiar to the Somerset & Dorset and not one found on Midland engines where the frames were similarly flush with the running plate and so offered no protection against any spillage reaching the motion. The tenders were similar to those provided for the Vulcan-built 0-6-0s, and like them were without coal rails. The dimensions were as follows:

Cylinders	18in × 24in
Bogie wheels	3ft 0in
Coupled wheels	5ft 9in
Wheelbase	6ft 0in + 6ft 6in + 8ft 3in = 20ft 9in
Boiler diameter	4ft 1in
Boiler length	10ft 0in
Firebox length	5ft 6in
Boiler pitch	7ft 0in
Heating surfaces:	*sq ft*
Tubes (246 × 1⅝in)	1,098
Firebox	104
Total	1,202
Working pressure	150lb
Grate area	16sq ft
Weight in working order:	*tons cwt*
Bogie	12 17
Leading coupled wheels	15 2
Trailing coupled wheels	11 1
Engine total	39 0
Tender (2,200gal)	29 18
Engine and tender	68 18

On 6 February 1895 two more, Nos 67 and 68, were ordered from Derby at a cost of £2,230 each while a second pair, Nos 14 and 45, at the same price, was authorised on 30 October 1895. The first two were delivered in January 1896 and the

second in February 1897. Visually the difference between these engines and Nos 15 to 18 concerned the sight-feed lubricator pipes which on the earlier series ran along below the cladding plates to reappear under the boiler barrel just to the rear of the smoke-box tubeplate. This was the system employed at the time of their construction on new Midland engines, but was not persisted with so that by the time Nos 14, 45, 67 and 68 were built there had been a return to the usual arrangement of utilising the left handrail. This was a much simpler and easier maintained alternative.

On 1 November 1886 the Wimborne avoiding line had been opened, an improvement necessitated by the continuous ex-pansion of traffic to and from Bournemouth throughout much of the year. Hitherto an inconvenient and time-wasting reversal had been necessary at Wimborne which involved the use of the London & South Western's station and the 2½ mile section to Broadstone over which all services from Southampton to Dor-chester or Weymouth were routed with inevitable delays to the Somerset & Dorset trains. The new line shortened the through journey by some three miles, although when Nos 15 to 18 took over the best expresses the overall Bath–Bournemouth timing was unchanged from that of 1880. The 2.25pm ex-Bath, with an extra stop at Evercreech Junction, was still allowed 1hr 45min to Blandford while the 5.45pm with four intermediate stops was scheduled to run the 63¾ miles to Broadstone in 2hr 6min. On the up journey the best train was the 9.40am ex-Bournemouth which reached Bath at 11.50am, the 31 miles between Blandford and Shepton Mallet being timed for 54min, the same as ten years earlier. However, there were improve-ments in the timing over the heavily graded Shepton Mallet–Bath section where the 21¾ miles were booked at 35min giving an average speed of 37¼mph for the 1.30pm ex-Bournemouth. It was over this length of track that the new 4-4-0s proved their worth and later when all were available there was a general tightening of schedules and an increase in loadings. So that by the turn of the century the best down expresses were timed at 2hr 10min to Bournemouth inclusive of seven intermediate stops, of which four were at South Western stations after Broadstone. During the intervening years working conditions had been materially eased by the doubling of much of the line between Bath and Templecombe, although to a large extent this had been nullified by the introduction of longer trains and very heavy electric-lighted Midland bogie stock together with Pullman cars on many excursions. Whitaker requested more 4-4-0s in April 1900, but in vain, and the eight in hand had to struggle on assisted by sundry 0-6-0s and bogie tanks for three more years.

Reboilering of the original series became necessary in 1904–6, but instead of taking advantage of this to fit a larger pattern, Derby supplied new boilers of similar size to those displaced. The barrel was of steel in three telescopic rings with the closed dome centrally placed and not as in the bogie tanks' replacement boilers where only two rings were employed. The Ramsbottom safety valves and an auxiliary lock-up valve over the firebox were contained in a large brass casing while the chimney was a tall pattern only found on Joint engines. The 240 1⅝in tubes were arranged Johnson fashion in horizontal rows while the heating surfaces were:

	sq ft
Tubes	1,072
Firebox	104
	1,176
Working pressure	160lb

Dates when reboilering occurred were: 1904: Nos 17 (August), 18 (December); 1905: No 15 (April); 1906: No 16 (April). At the same time most engines received a new toolbox with curved ends placed across and over the coal space at the tender front, this being a feature introduced on a limited scale by the Midland in 1902.

The continued use of small boilers by Derby ceased in 1904 when a start was made in fitting a much larger pattern. Credit for this is invariably assigned to Deeley, although the scheme in fact was instigated by Johnson in November 1903 just prior to his retirement. On the Somerset & Dorset the need for greater boiler power was apparently not considered urgent for it was 1907 before a start was made rejuvenating Nos 14 to 18, 45, 67 and 68 with boilers of the Johnson H pattern with the barrel shortened by 6in to accommodate the framing of the smaller wheelbased Joint 4-4-os. Some had the Deeley vertical rowed tube layout while all had Johnson's final 1902 pattern smoke-box door with central hand wheel and strap hinges. No 67 in October 1907 was the first reboilered, dates of the others being: 1908: No 68 (July); 1909: No 45 (August); 1910: Nos 14 (December), 15 (September), 16 (April), 17 (January); 1911: No 18 (June). Derby supplied the boilers, that fitted to No 67 having been in stock since 1904, and had the tubes arranged in horizontal rows whereas those allotted to Nos 17, 45 and 68 followed Deeley practice by having them arranged vertically. Nos 14, 15, 16, and 18 reverted to the earlier layout in order to make use of tubeplates lying in stock from the Johnson era. Besides having shorter barrels, these eight boilers also differed from the genuine article by having the dome sited towards the rear of the foremost ring and only about 3ft 6in behind the tubeplate which gave a hump-backed appearance. No 67 had its Ramsbottom safety valves and auxiliary lock-up valve en-closed in a large brass casing, whereas the others had theirs fully exposed. At first short Johnson flowerpot chimneys with Deeley capuchons were carried, but later these were discarded in favour of a parallel variety. The dimensions of these boilers were:

Diameter		4ft 8in	
Length		10ft 0in	
Firebox length		7ft 0in	
Pitch		8ft 0in	
	No 67	*Nos 17, 45, 68*	*Nos 14, 15, 16, 18*
Number of tubes			
(1¾in)	256	242	258
Heating surfaces:	*sq ft*	*sq ft*	*sq ft*
Tubes	1,219	1,157	1,228

Firebox	125	125	125
Total	1,344	1,282	1,353

Grate area	21·1sq ft
Working pressure	160lb

The working order weight was increased to:

	tons	cwt
Bogie	14	8
Leading coupled wheels	16	6
Trailing coupled wheels	15	14
Engine total	46	8
Tender (2,600gal)	32	18
Engine and tender	79	6

To take the larger boiler the frames were lengthened at the rear of the trailing coupled wheels while the cab with its arched roof and pillars was of a pattern midway between that employed by Johnson on his larger-boilered designs and that of Deeley's final type. The original tenders were enlarged to carry 2,600gal.

After this reboiling these eight engines were comparable in size and power with Nos 69 to 71, 77 and 78 of 1903–8. The latter carried full length 'H' or 'H1' pattern boilers and were also much newer, but nevertheless the men never thought so well of them and whenever possible chose the older engines for the hardest express services until the arrival of the superheated 4-4-0s. Since the former in many cases lasted until LMS days whereas the 1903 trio had all disappeared by 1921 the men's views were undoubtedly correct.

The 1904–6 boilers removed from Nos 15 to 18 were repaired and transferred to Fowler goods Nos 24, 23, 19 and 22 respectively.

The Whitaker tablet-exchanging apparatus came into general service at nine main line stations on 1 January 1904 after some years of test operation on the Bridgwater branch. This materially

eased the working of the single sections of track by removing the
necessity of making large reductions in speed whenever tablets
had to be picked up or dropped. The cost was remarkably low
considering the time saved and injuries avoided, it being just
£245 to equip seventy-one engines and to provide nine stations
with the necessary apparatus. A further, and to the passengers
a much more important, improvement came in February 1906
when carriage-heating equipment was fitted to Nos 16, 45 and
68, and large 4-4-0 No 71 at a cost of £116 in order that they
could be rostered for the best Bath–Bournemouth expresses.
For some years the Midland through coaches had been equipped for steam heating, but hitherto on the Somerset & Dorset
no use could be made of it and resort had to be made to foot-
warmers. Joint crews never liked steam heating—there was
little enough steam to spare without it. The normal practice was
to turn it on full while standing in Bath and then switch it off on
the journey southwards until about Midford. Presumably there
was a similar system for the trains from Bournemouth.

Nos 67 and 68 were withdrawn in 1920–1 and replaced by
two superheated 4-4-0s, but the other six worked on although
relegated to less exacting tasks. No 45 in September 1926 was
fitted with a shortened G7 Belpaire boiler which necessitated
the raising of the upper part of the cab and its widening out
beyond the splasher faces. The roof was also extended, but the
circular look-out windows were retained. No 17 was similarly
reboilered in November 1927 and in addition was provided
with new frames having a greater depth between the smokebox
and the driving splashers, the top edge being level with the
base of the smokebox. Both engines carried Deeley parallel
chimneys, that on No 45 being slightly longer. Changed
dimensions were as follows:

Heating surfaces:	*sq ft*
Tubes (252 × 1¾in)	1,199½
Firebox	127
Total	1,326½

Weight in working order:	tons	cwt
Bogie	14	7
Leading coupled wheels	17	7
Trailing coupled wheels	15	8
Total	47	2

The result was not entirely successful for the shortness of the barrel in relation to the firebox and the proportion of the tube diameter to the length made both engines very heavy on fuel and water when worked hard. On the other hand they were unusually free steaming.

In August 1928 Nos 15 and 16 were condemned while in the same month No 18 was renumbered 15 and Belpaire No 45 altered to 18. Blue had been the standard passenger livery since 1886, but in October 1929 a change was made to black, probably with the coming transfer of ownership in mind. Only one engine, No 18, actually appeared in the new colours before the end of the year. The four survivors, Nos 14, 15, 17 and 18, were allotted Nos 300 to 303 by the LMS, although No 14 was laid aside before the change occurred. With so many suitable replacements to hand, little time was lost in withdrawing the other three, the last to go being Belpaire No 303 in February 1932, with a mileage of 786,943.

CHAPTER SIX

THE LARGE 4-4-0s

After presenting his report to the managing committee in January 1900 Whitaker criticised the performance of the eight small 4-4-0s supplied by Derby for express service during the previous nine years. Experience had shown them incapable of working unaided many of the line's passenger services, even over the relatively easy section south of Evercreech Junction. Indeed, many of the delays afflicted on the unfortunate passengers throughout the summer months could be attributed to water, and sometimes coal also, having to be taken at Templecombe. In recent years the operating and maintenance costs had risen steeply while the coal consumption at 47lb per mile was some 30 per cent greater than that recorded by similar-sized engines on the Midland main line. Whitaker's standing at Derby and Highbridge was such that his views were accepted, but nevertheless no immediate action was taken because of lack of funds and it was only after a worsening of the operational difficulties in 1902 that authorisation was granted on 6 August for the supply of three larger 4-4-0s by Derby at a cost of £3,500 each. Delivery was requested before the following Easter and when this could not be promised attempts were made to have their construction transferred to Nine Elms Works (LSWR) or to an outside contractor. Dugald Drummond, with characteristic crustiness, adamantly refused any adjustment of the South Western's building programme and when no reputable manufacturer could be found to accept the order at such short notice, Derby was obliged to grant some measure of priority. But for all that they were not completed until November 1903, when they were immediately set to work on the best express services.

They were impressively handsome engines and of considerably larger dimensions than the earlier Johnson 4-4-0s, although still not over-powerful for heavy passenger duty over the taxing Somerset & Dorset line. Similar engines on the Midland Railway were regarded as rebuilds of 4-4-0s originally carrying small 4ft 1in boilers, but Nos 69 to 71 were booked out new. Their dimensions were as follows:

Cylinders	18in × 26in
Bogie	3ft 1in
Coupled wheels	6ft 0in
Wheelbase	6ft 0in + 7ft 0½in + 8ft 6in = 21ft 6½in
Boiler diameter	4ft 8in
Boiler length	10ft 6in
Firebox length	7ft 0in
Boiler pitch	8ft 0in
Heating surfaces:	*sq ft*
Tubes (258 × 1¾in)	1,295
Firebox	125
Total	1,420
Grate area	21·1sq ft
Working pressure	175lb

Weight in working order:	*tons*	*cwt*
Bogie	15	9
Leading coupled wheels	16	9
Trailing coupled wheels	14	6
Engine total	46	4
Tender (2,950gal)	35	2
Engine and tender	81	6

From the above it will be noted that the increase in power was relative only, the real improvement over the earlier small-boilered engines being in the steaming capacity and higher working pressure. Johnson did not retire until the end of 1903 so Nos 69 to 71 were to his design and carried the standard 'H' pattern boiler with the tubes laid out in horizontal rows and a closed dome on the rearmost of two rings. There were three safety valves over the firebox contained in a large brass casing, the rearmost consisted of a pair of Ramsbottom valves with a spring between adjusted to 175lb while the foremost was a single lock-up valve of smaller diameter adjusted to 180lb. The bogie, valve gear, lifting combination pattern injectors and steam sanding equipment all followed previous Derby practice as on the earlier 4-4-os while they also followed the latter in contra-distinction to current Derby 4-4-0 practice by having plate springs for the leading coupled wheels. The brake gear similarly conformed with that of the earlier 4-4-os, though like o-6-os Nos 72 to 76 the steam cylinder was horizontal.

Features new to the line, other than the boiler with its short flowerpot chimney and the final Johnson cab, included fluted coupling rods, a straight cut top to the frames from the smoke-box front to the leading buffer beam, strap type smokebox door hinges and U-brackets for the brake hangers.

Two generally similar engines, Nos 77 and 78, were ordered from Derby at £3,375 each on 8 May 1907. Whitaker had asked for three powerful passenger and six eight-coupled goods engines on 10 January 1907, but at the next directors' meeting this request was refused because £34,700 would be necessary to strengthen three bridges and two stretches of permanent way before heavier engines could be used. However, they did promise that all future track and bridge renewals would be made with this in mind.

Nos 77 and 78 had Deeley cabs, H1 boilers, well-proportioned chimneys, a simpler safety valve layout without the large casing, no brass splasher beading, and smokebox doors having strap hinges and secured by clips and bolts. Nos 69 to 71, of course, had Johnson's final type of door with a central handwheel. There was also a new straight form of handrailing on the smoke-box door with the side handrailing stopping-off near the smokebox front, both features being destined for perpetuation not only on the Midland but also by the LMS.

The overall dimensions and many structural features of their boilers followed those of the earlier engines, although in accordance with Deeley's preference the tubes were arranged in vertical rows. The heating surfaces were:

	sq ft
Tubes (242 × 1¾in)	1,222
Firebox	125
Total	1,347

Weight in working order:	tons	cwt
Bogie	15	10
Leading coupled wheels	16	12
Trailing coupled wheels	15	6
Engine total	47	8
Tender (2,950gal)	36	13
Engine and tender	84	1

The Johnson tenders, like those of Nos 69 to 71, had large slots in the frames and coal rails. They must, however, have been more heavily constructed because they weighed some 1½ tons more, though the capacity was unchanged.

In general service the drivers found these five engines very capable and a great improvement on the smaller 4-4-os before the latter received shortened H boilers, but praise from the firemen was not so forthcoming as they had to satisfy their voracious appetites for coal. In particular they had little regard for the 1903 trio and much preferred firing the earlier 4-4-os after the fitting of larger boilers in 1907–11, especially when the weight of trains approached that permissible without resorting to double heading. Should the boilers of these three engines be at all dirty then there was a tendency to prime while hot driving boxes caused trouble for some years. Whitaker considered the driving wheels at 6ft oin too large for Somerset & Dorset conditions and would have preferred the 5ft 9in diameter of the original 4-4-o series. In the light of modern knowledge on the subject this was obviously invalid, but at the time, and for many years thereafter, there was a strongly held belief that the choice of driving wheel diameter for a locomotive was a matter of critical importance. In the technical literature of the period it can be discerned that a locomotive engineer of exceptional genius could achieve a near-miracle by calculating to the last half inch the ideal wheel diameter. No thoughts were given to the fact that changes of three inches or so could be made to this critical figure by routine machining of the tyres until they became too thin for further service. Presumably such diameter changes were conveniently forgotten. Whitaker undoubtedly was on the wrong tack here, but the coal returns for the half year ending 31 December 1908 fully confirm the firemen's criticism.

Engine No	Time out of shops (months)	Coal burnt per mile (lb)
69	11	48·7
70	14	49·2
71	3	48·9
77	new engine	47·4
78	,, ,,	46·8
70*	,, ,,	37·2

* Superheated '483' class of 1914.

The oil consumption of Nos 69 to 71 was unusually heavy while 77 and 78 were reputed to suffer badly from flats on the coupled wheels.

During the years preceding World War I the popularity of Bournemouth and the New Forest for holidays rapidly increased, and since many of the visitors lived in the Midlands or North Country they travelled via the Somerset & Dorset. This, together with the use of much heavy Midland Railway coaching stock, made double heading or banking necessary for most summer expresses and excursions which raised the operating costs above that desirable. As a result, in April 1911 Derby sent Deeley Flat-iron 0-6-4 tank No 2023 to Bath for trials on the heaviest passenger duties. There was no lack of power, but the unsteadiness and oscillation at anything above moderate speeds and the restricted tank capacity proved so disadvantageous that it was returned home and in the spring of 1913 483 class superheated 4-4-0 No 499 was sent in exchange. It gave a much better account of itself and before long was joined by No 519 of the same class. Both were returned to the Midland in the autumn and orders given for the withdrawal of Nos 69 and 70, and their replacement by two superheated 4-4-0s of similar design. Later the frames of No 71 were found in such poor condition that it was substituted for No 69 which was repaired and returned to traffic unaltered. The Midland Railway always considered its 483 class as rebuilds of earlier and smaller 4-4-0s, although with their new frames and cylinders, and Schmidt superheated G7 boilers, there could have remained very little of the old engines when returned to traffic. The first rebuild was No 494 (ex-No 153) of February 1912 while ultimately there were no less than 157 Midland and 5 Somerset & Dorset members of the class. At Highbridge, however, all such engines were recorded as new.

With mileages of 266,017 and 247,242 respectively the boilers from the replaced engines were salvaged and after being fitted with new fireboxes were transferred to Bulldog 0-6-0s Nos 63 and 66. This made these two engines, apart from the 2-8-0s, the most powerful engines on the line and very useful for passenger workings during the summer months.

The remaining 1903 4-4-0, No 69, was scheduled for similar replacement in 1916, but because of World War I this had to be postponed until April 1921 when the mileage totalled 344,192. At the same time small 5ft 9in 4-4-0s Nos 67 and 68 were taken out of traffic and sent to Derby from whence they, too, emerged as members of the 483 class.

They were attractive looking 4-4-0s and with their high pitched G7S boiler, Belpaire firebox, slightly extended smoke-box, Fowler chimney, raised running plate to clear the coupled wheels and neat cab had all the characteristics of later Midland practice. The superheater was of the Schmidt type and consisted of 21 × 5$\frac{1}{8}$in elements while the 8in piston valves were below the cylinders in the style adopted by Johnson for passenger engines in 1897. The Stephenson valve gear similarly followed current Derby practice as did the braking layout with its central pull-rods and vacuum-controlled steam brake cylinder under the drag-plate. The bogie was also equipped with brake shoes between the pairs of wheels, each side being operated directly from a 'floating' brake cylinder hung between them. The dimensions were as follows:

Cylinders	20$\frac{1}{2}$in × 26in
Bogie	3ft 6$\frac{1}{2}$in
Coupled wheels	7ft 0$\frac{1}{2}$in
Wheelbase	6ft 0in + 7ft 2$\frac{1}{2}$in + 9ft 6in = 22ft 8$\frac{1}{2}$in
Boiler diameter	4ft 8in
Boiler length	10ft 5$\frac{13}{16}$in
Firebox length	7ft 0in
Boiler pitch	8ft 6$\frac{1}{4}$in
Heating surfaces:	*sq ft*
Tubes (148 × 1$\frac{3}{4}$in, 21 × 5$\frac{1}{8}$in)	1,045
Firebox	125
Total	1,170
Superheater	313sq ft
Grate area	21·1sq ft
Working pressure	160lb

Weight in working order:	*tons*	*cwt*
Bogie	18	18
Leading coupled wheels	17	10
Trailing coupled wheels	16	19
Engine total	53	7
Tender (3,250gal)	37	0
Engine and tender	90	7

The costs of these engines make interesting reading for being dispatched to traffic both before and after World War I they fully illustrate the escalation of building expenses during the intervening years.

Engine No	Date	Cost		
		Engine	Tender	Total
		£	£	£
70	May 1914	2,269	577	2,846
71	April 1914	2,250	585	2,835
67	April 1921	6,483	1,647	8,130
68	,,	,,	,,	,,
69	,,	5,995	1,630	7,625

The tenders were Somerset & Dorset property so presumably there was no actual charge for them. Like those coupled to most of the Midland 483 rebuilds they held 3,250gal of water and 4 tons of coal. Nos 70 and 71 received their tenders from Bull-dog 0-6-os Nos 72 and 75 while those attached to the 1921 series had similarly seen service behind Nos 73, 74 and 76.

The primary advantage of superheating lay in the economy of fuel and water, although also of importance was the frac-tionally swifter movement of superheated steam which made engines employing it marginally faster than those using the saturated commodity. In traffic therefore these five superheated 4-4-os proved more lively than the large saturated engines and averaged only 37lb of coal per mile as against their 48 to 49lb. However, no superheater offered any advantage until an engine had been working long and hard enough to get a really hot fire. On the Somerset & Dorset there were no fears of this for all main line expresses required really hard driving. The difficulty was to keep the firebox well topped with fuel, so that the fierce blast ensured that the coal was a permanent incandescent white hot mass. At night the large saturated 4-4-os were an amazing sight when being well and truly thrashed with a 'jimmy' across the blast pipe to sharpen the exhaust. The lower section of the smokebox door would be red hot and the exhaust one long solid column of fire and sparks. This never happened with the superheated engines—they seldom fire-threw or gave off clouds of black smoke unless the coal was of particularly poor quality.

As previously mentioned No 67 to 71, like all Midland classes of the twentieth century, were under-powered for the heaviest passenger duties. Their loading, for instance, over the Bath–Evercreech section with its 1 in 50 grades was restricted to 212 tons which could hardly eliminate piloting in the summer months. Indeed, later this was reduced to 190 tons, that is to say, only a single carriage more than the earlier 4-4-0s. On the credit side, however, they were cheap and easy to maintain since Derby had paid special attention to good lubrication, the use of robustly designed fittings and the provision of adequate bearing surfaces. Coal consumption was moderate for the ruggedly designed short travel valve gear permitted accurate timing while the boiler was well endowed with grate area and gave a respectable rate of combustion. It is probably fair to say that these engines were reasonably well suited to Somerset & Dorset conditions provided the maintenance was of a high order and their limitations appreciated.

In the *Railway Magazine* Cecil J. Allen once wrote: 'Except on the steep banks, the running last Summer on the Somerset & Dorset was entirely devoid of interest; the schedules were easy and time was almost invariably lost by the locomotives.' Apparently other observers must have harboured similar thoughts since very little has been recorded of the line's loco-motive performance before 1920. Those that follow have been collected mainly from the *Railway Magazine* and *Railway and Travel Monthly.*

The departure from Bath (Midland Railway) was level to the Junction from whence the line climbed for 2 miles at 1 in 50, apart from a stretch of level between the ¾ and 1 mile posts. From there to Radstock the gradients were slightly more favourable although still requiring skilful driving and an adequate supply of steam, while thence to the 17¾ mile post just before Masbury the Mendips themselves had to be tackled. The first mile rose at grades varying between 1 in 55 and 1 in

THE FOWLER GOODS ENGINES

Page 101   (*Top*) 0-6-0 No 21 in original condition. Note the domeless boiler and cast number plate. (*Bottom*) 0-6-0 No 19 as rebuilt in 1888. The safety valve and dome covers are not fitted but note the new cast number plate

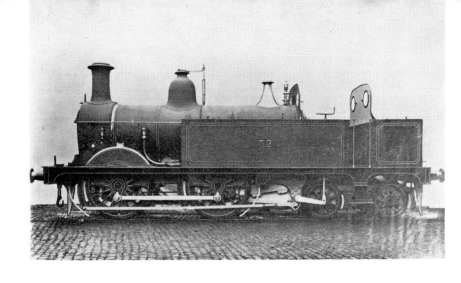

THE AVONSIDE TANKS

Page 102 (*Top*) 0-4-4T No 32 as built in 1877. (*Bottom*) 0-4-4T No 30 as reboilered in 1906 but with later Deeley-style chimney and smokebox door. This locomotive was renumbered 30A in 1926 and for a time was fitted for push-pull working. It became LMS No 1206 in 1930 and was withdrawn in 1932

100 which then hardened to 1 in 50 for a mile to Midsomer Norton. Here a break at 1 in 300 occurred for the length of the station before the ascent continued at 1 in 58 and 60 for the 2 miles to Chilcompton where a similar brief easing of the gradient took place before a final mile at 1 in 50. The remaining section to Masbury was less severe, although including a mile of 1 in 67 and 70 from the $15\frac{1}{4}$ mile post and another of 1 in 83 steepening to 1 in 73.

These five runs over this section are the best found for the 1914–15 period, but very probably do not adequately show the classes concerned at their best.

Engine No		18	78	66	70	71
Class		5ft 9in	6ft 0in	5ft 3in	7ft 0in	7ft 0in
		4-4-0	Saturated	0-6-0	Superheated	Superheated
		H1 Boiler	4-4-0	H Boiler	4-4-0	4-4-0
Load		110 tons	131 tons	178 tons	204 tons	191 tons
Wind		Light	Moderate	Calm	Calm	Light
		Westerly	Easterly			South-West
Miles	From Bath (MR)	Min Sec	Min Sec	Min Sec	Min Sec	Min Sec
$\frac{1}{4}$	Bath Junction	00 38*	01 52	01 48	01 45	01 50
$2\frac{1}{4}$	MP 2	06 00	06 53	06 47	07 20	06 49
$4\frac{3}{8}$	Midford	08 53	09 49	09 40	10 35	09 41
$10\frac{1}{2}$	MP 10	17 53	19 19	18 09	20 08	19 01
$10\frac{5}{8}$	Radstock	—	—	18 55	—	—
$12\frac{1}{4}$	Midsomer Norton	22 23	24 07	05 31	25 45	23 57
$14\frac{1}{2}$	Chilcompton	27 27	29 32	11 23	31 47	29 17
17	Binegar	33 08	34 29	17 00	37 24	34 01
$18\frac{1}{4}$	MP $17\frac{3}{4}$	35 54	36 51	19 11	39 51	36 16
$18\frac{5}{8}$	Masbury	—	37 27	19 41	40 28	36 50
$21\frac{7}{8}$	Shepton Mallet	41 12	41 57	23 59	44 20	41 11

NB—The mile posts on the Somerset & Dorset are measured from Bath Junction.
* Started 5 chains from the Junction.

The two superheater engines easily gave the most impressive performance, but that by the large-boilered 0-6-0 No 66 was approaching the same standard. No wonder that this engine, and the similarly reboilered No 63, was regularly rostered for such services before the Armstrongs entered traffic in 1922.

In the reverse direction the climb from Evercreech Junction to Masbury summit necessitated similar periods of sustained

D

hard slogging, and again from those logs available the super-heated 4-4-0s came out best, details being as follows:

Engine No	Load (tons)	7/8 mile to 25 MP, and 1/2 mile up 1 in 50 to 22 MP							22 MP pass		Shepton Mallet		17 1/4 MP pass	
		sec	sec	sec	sec	sec	sec	sec	min	sec	min	sec	min	sec
78 (a)	153	169	59	74	86	95	92	95	11	10	12	50	9	58
70 (b)	157	163	53	64	75	84	87	93	10	19	12	11	9	33
78 (a)	165	182	61	78	89	95	97	99	11	41	13	22	10	20

(a) 6ft 0in saturated 4-4-0. (b) 7ft 0in superheated 4-4-0

The work demanded daily of these engines was particularly taxing no matter in which direction they were bound, for of necessity the regulator had to be closed going down hills immediately following a sustained spell of hard pounding to reach the summit of the various banks. This gave rise to sudden variations of temperature in the steam passages which greatly added to maintenance difficulties, especially with the superheated engines. Another problem was caused by the difference in water depths over the firebox crown consequent on passing over the various summits. Climbing up hill the water level at the firebox end would be about two inches higher than it would be when the engine was running on level track whereas when over the summit and on a falling gradient the level would be some two inches lower. The crew, therefore, must ensure that more water was carried in the boiler whilst climbing than would be necessary if a stop could be made at the summit and the boiler topped up before commencing the run down hill. All hill work had to be undertaken with this in mind and care taken not to let the boiler level fall excessively in order to conserve steam.

The coal crisis of 1921 led to the government requesting all main line railways to convert locomotives to oil-firing, but because of the expense and the time taken to assemble the necessary fittings only 116 had been modified before the coal industry was able to offer improved supplies. Oil had not proved as cheap or versatile as coal so engines were rapidly taken out of traffic for reconversion. On the Midland Fowler devised his own oil-burning equipment which was cheaper and much simpler than any of the better known patent systems. No alteration was necessary to the firebox beyond the lining of the front tube plate below the arch with a fire brick wall, and as the burner or burners were attached to the fire hole, no special openings were required between the inner and outer firebox sheets. Provision was made for small-scale coal firing, but this seldom proved necessary as it was generally possible to run entirely on oil, the whole of the firebars being covered with brick fragments. When lighting up from cold a pressure of about 40lb was raised by a wood fire before the oil burners were brought into use. The burners resembled the Mexican Trough type, but were simpler and less liable to clog. The oil emerged in a ribbon-like stream from the top of the apparatus to be atomised by contact with a steam jet coming from below, the flame stream being directed forwards and downwards to the incandescent covering of brick fragments on the grate. Two cylindrical drums or tanks holding 450gal each were mounted on the tender without any means for preliminary warming of the oil, which had a flash-point of 170–80° F.

On 15 June 1921 two sets of equipment were ordered to be dispatched to Highbridge, these being followed by four more later in the month for the intention was to convert 4-4-0s Nos 67 to 69 and 2-8-0s Nos 81, 84 and 85. It is known that Nos 67, 68 and 84 were dealt with in August 1921, but no mention is made in the repair register of the other three engines. Apparently the two 4-4-0s were employed on the best expresses with some success, although their progress across Somerset could be followed by a pall of black smoke and a large pile of chopped up sleepers had to be carried in the tender in case the fire went out while standing in stations. After a long run it was not unknown for oil to be dripping off the roof of the leading coach. No 84 was reconverted to coal after only a few weeks so presumably was less satisfactory.

Despite the success of the superheated engines the remaining two 6ft 0in 4-4-0s, Nos 77 and 78, were not withdrawn or replaced in similar fashion, but left to work out their time using saturated steam. When new boilers became necessary they were supplied with the Midland G7 pattern having Belpaire fire-boxes, No 78 in November 1921 and No 77 in May 1926. Other visual changes included rectangular look-out windows, the widening of the cab to suit the Belpaire firebox and a lowering of the dome cover. The additional footsteps and handrailing abreast of the rear bogie wheels had been fitted while still carry-ing the 'H1' boiler. Earlier in February–March 1921 their 2,950gal tenders were transferred to Bulldog 0-6-0s Nos 73 and 76, and in exchange received the enlarged tenders left surplus by the withdrawn 5ft 9in Johnson 4-4-0s Nos 67 and 68. Changed dimensions were as follows:

Heating surfaces:	*sq ft*	
Tubes (252 × 1¾in)	1,257	
Firebox	127	
Total	1,384	

Weight in working order:	*tons*	*cwt*
Bogie	15	18
Leading coupled wheels	17	3
Trailing coupled wheels	15	8
Engine total	48	9
Tender (2,600gal)	35	13
Engine and tender	84	2

Both engines entered LMS stock when they were renumbered 320 and 321. At the time the former retained the blue livery from which the Joint crest, cabside numerals and tender initials had been blanked out and replaced by LMS insignia. The new number was also painted on the smokebox door below the handrailing. No 321 was under repair in January 1930 and when dispatched to traffic was LMS black with a cast-iron smoke-box numberplate. Still blue, No 320 was condemned in Septem-ber 1931, but its companion received a standard Midland

2,950gal tender at Derby in June 1933 and was overhauled at Bow Works in March 1936 before finally succumbing in March 1938. It had remained working on the Somerset & Dorset until October 1934 when a move was made to Burton and from where it was occasionally employed piloting a Claughton between Leicester and Leeds on the down *Thames–Clyde* express.

The delivery of Nos 67 to 69 in April 1921 only gave the line five modern superheated 4-4-os which patently was too few for the winter let alone the holiday months of summer. Nevertheless, all requests for more express locomotives fell on deaf ears until May 1928 when authorisation was given for the purchase of three Fowler LMS Class 2 4-4-os at £5,000 each. This long delay was the result of economies brought into force by an inquiry conducted in 1921 to investigate working losses of £64,000 and £71,000 respectively suffered during the two preceding years. Many of the measures to save money could be applied at once, but others were of longer term so it was the end of 1926 before the annual deficit could be reduced to a more acceptable £6,000. Under these circumstances it was not surprising that only the five versatile Armstrong o-6-os and a second batch of 2-8-os were added stock between 1922 and 1928. The LMS, however, did give trials to several classes during the 1925–7 period, the first to arrive being Deeley Class 990 4-4-0 No 995 (coupled to tender No 1060) in August and September 1925 while Horwich 2-6-0 No 13064 followed in November 1927. The former was well liked by the men, but showed little advantage over Nos 67 to 71 and burnt considerably more fuel in so doing. On one occasion it failed about half a mile from Masbury summit with a southbound excursion when the regulator refused to open fully. The 2-6-0 did remarkably well on the passenger services, and reasonably proficiently on the goods, and was returned with such glowing reports that all concerned imagined the next passenger engines would be of that class. News of the Fowler 4-4-os therefore came as an unwelcome surprise to the hard-pressed crews who rightly considered the steep gradients called for six-coupled wheels.

In 1928 Fowler 4-4-os were being built for the LMS. Therefore, on receipt of instructions to supply three to Highbridge, Derby transferred Nos 575, 576 and 580 as s & djr Nos 44 to 46. All were painted blue, although the first two had been run-in on the Derby–Birmingham semi-fasts as lms Nos 575 and 576 before being renumbered. When ordered £5,000 had been the asking price, but this was later reduced to £4,320 each to compensate Highbridge for various secondhand boilers and other materials disposed of by Derby as scrap. Their dimensions were as follows:

Cylinders	19in × 26in
Bogie	3ft 6½in
Coupled wheels	6ft 9in
Wheelbase	6ft 0in + 7ft 2½in + 9ft 6in = 22ft 8½in
Boiler diameter	4ft 8in
Boiler length	10ft 5$\frac{15}{16}$in
Firebox length	7ft 0in
Boiler pitch	8ft 6in
Heating surfaces:	*sq ft*
Tubes (146 × 1¾in and 21 × 5⅛in)	1,034
Firebox	124
Total	1,158
Superheater	253sq ft
Grate area	21·1sq ft
Working pressure	180lb

Weight in working order:	tons	cwt
Bogie	19	2
Leading coupled wheels	17	15
Trailing coupled wheels	17	4
Engine total	54	1
Tender (3,500gal)	41	4
Engine and tender	95	5

They were essentially similar to the 1921 series, although incorporating various modifications introduced by the lms.

These principally concerned the cylinders, coupled wheels and
working pressure; the first mentioned being 1½in less in diameter,
the coupled wheels smaller by 3in and the working pressure
raised to 180lb. More noticeable were the lower dome and
chimney, the left-hand drive, the Ross pop safety valves and the
modernised, straight-sided tender with solid plate coal fenders.
Sanding remained by steam, but extra containers supplied sand
to the front of the trailing coupled wheels. The design was neat
and attractive, although, of course, being far too small for the
main line duties expected of these engines daily on the Somerset & Dorset. However, considering the LMS was satisfied with
building Compounds for the important and heavy Scottish
expresses until 1927, it could hardly be expected that requests
for six-coupled engines from the Highbridge outpost would fall
on sympathetic ears. However, with characteristic ingenuity
Joint foremen overcame this deficiency by rostering a superheated 4-4-0 and an Armstrong goods for the heaviest expresses.
Together they formed a truly formidable source of power,
albeit at the expense of four wages and a coal consumption
approaching 90lb per mile.

Returning to the earlier superheated engines, Nos 67 to 71
were renumbered 39 to 43 in August 1928. This was undertaken
by attaching small rectangular metal plates showing the new
numbers to the cab side-sheets and removing the cast-iron
smokebox door number plates. Under LMS ownership in 1930
they became Nos 322 to 326 and thereby filled vacancies in that
company's list just prior to similar ex-Midland Railway 4-4-0s.
All were still blue, excepting No 322 which, being away at
Derby for general overhaul, was returned not only renumbered
but also painted black. Previously it had been standard practice
for engines to retain their own boilers despite consequent delays
in shops, but now regular boiler exchanges were made so No
322 returned in May 1930 with the boiler removed from LMS
No 547. Other changes made over the next few years included
the removal of the bogie brakes and the Fowler–Anderson by-
pass valves, and the addition of air-relief valves. Later Stanier-
pattern chimneys made an appearance.

In 1930 Nos 44 to 46 became LMS Nos 633 to 635, it not being possible for them to retake their original LMS numbers because these had been filled earlier by three replacement engines. Nos 634 and 635 retained the blue livery with the Joint line's insignia blanked out and that of the LMS superimposed, the smokebox door number plates painted over and their new numbers inscribed below in white. No 633, however, was in shops and came out black. At this period Dabeg feed water heaters were being considered by the LMS and fitted experimentally to a number of locomotives, and in November 1933 No 633 was added to this select band. The cost, including the necessary minor modifications to the steam and feed water piping, was £425. The pump was mounted on the left-hand platform adjacent to the smokebox, the drive being obtained by a crank from the driving crank pin and a lever through a rocking arm pivoted at platform level. It was divided into two sections, one for hot and the other for cold water, with the right to left movement of the ram in the latter drawing feed water from the tender and the reverse movement delivering it upwards to the condenser. Here the water dropped through the exhaust steam, gained heat and was then drawn out of the condenser to the hot water compartment from whence delivery to the boiler was made via a clack on the left side of the barrel. When the regulator was closed an automatic feed valve prevented any water entering the condenser while the water flow could be governed by a cock on the driver's side of the footplate from where a rod passed directly to the front end of the platform. An ordinary live steam injector was also carried, but the exhaust steam injector previously fitted was discarded. The Dabeg Company claimed reduced fuel and water consumption, a saving on boiler maintenance and longer periods between successive washouts, but in general service with many crews sharing engines the LMS found the savings insufficient to cover the purchase price. So the apparatus was not adopted, that on No 633 being kept until withdrawal.

After 1930 there was no longer any need to keep these eight engines on the Somerset & Dorset, but it was June 1936 before Nos 322/3/4 were transferred away to Millhouses and 325/6 to Saltley, and mid-1937 when Nos 633 to 635 went to Gloucester. Until 1938 their place on the line was filled by other LMS Class 2PS, including Nos 600/1/2, 699 and 700, but then Class 5 4-6-0s were allocated to Bath for the heaviest duties. This did not mean, however, the end of 4-4-0 usage on the Somerset & Dorset for the 2PS fulfilled a secondary role for many years to come. Later Nos 326 and 634 returned to the line, but the others were seen no more and over the years worked from such sheds as Skipton, Rhyl, Toton, Stafford, Burton and Llandudno Junction. The older engines were withdrawn in 1951-6, by which time Nos 40322 and 40323 had amassed mileages of 1,012,139 and 1,110,365 respectively, while Nos 40633 to 40635 lasted until 1959-62.

CHAPTER SEVEN

THE GOODS LOCOMOTIVES AND
SERVICES, 1875 to 1905

As with most English railways serving as common carriers, goods traffic in the decades before World War I was the very essence of Somerset & Dorset economy. By mid-1877 there were five daily goods over the old main line, of which three ran from Burnham to Templecombe and two right through to Wimborne, while the Bath Extension was provided with six trains daily together with a mineral train from Radstock and one conveying stone from the quarries at Binegar or Winsor Hill. The most important down goods left Bath at 10am with wagons from the Midland Railways 4.45 and 9.40am arrivals from the North and Gloucester. At Templecombe connections were made with South Western services to and from Exeter and the West, Salisbury, Bishopstoke, Portsmouth and Basingstoke, while the 7.18pm Wimborne arrival gave time for the transfer of wagons to the 8.10pm Southampton and Brockenhurst goods. In the reverse direction there was a similarly lavish provision of services with pride of place going to the 8.30pm through working from Bournemouth which regularly loaded to 35 wagons as far as Evercreech and thence 26 with banking assistance to Bath. Arrival at 5am was scheduled to offer connections with the Midland Railway's 7.25 and 10.05am departures to Bristol, Gloucester and the North.

The handling of heavy, loosely coupled goods trains over the steeply graded Bath Extension with braking assistance only available from the engine, tender and guards van was always a serious problem before the advent of the 2-8-0s in 1914. The golden rule was to pass the summits of Masbury and Cannards Grave as slowly as possible and then gradually increase the engine's speed as gravity accelerated the train. But with variations of crews the occasion would occur when somebody stormed over these summits at 20mph so that by the time the bottom of the dip was reached no engine on the line could either keep ahead of its train or stop. All couplings were, therefore, hanging slack and as soon as the next upgrade was struck there was one almighty tearing jerk which just about flung the crew through the spectacle plate and ten to one broke a coupling or drawbar. At the rear end the guard with his brake screwed up hard frequently had the floor boards afire and by the end of the journey must have wondered whether he was hired as a guard or a fire-brigade. As a result break-aways became common and the management was forced to step in and insist that a proportion of the wagon brakes was pinned down at Masbury and Cannards Grave summits. There was then some improvement, but it was not until some bold character forced his will upon the conservative majority and came practically to a stand at the foot of the banks, picked up the couplings gently from rest and reached his destination intact and to time that break-aways became infrequent and not daily occurrences.

With only the six Fowler 0-6-0s available for heavy main line service in 1875 it was obvious to the Derby inspection team that additional goods engines were urgently required. As a temporary measure Midland 0-6-0s Nos 351 and 353 were loaned in December 1875 while in May 1877 tenders were sought for the construction of six 0-6-0s of Johnson design. These were read over by the managing committee on 22 June 1877 when the offer of £2,275 each by Neilson & Co was accepted, delivery being promised by mid-1878. Apparently difficulty was met in keeping this date since in March 1878 Neilsons wrote requesting permission to sub-contract the construction of the boilers and tenders. At first the directors refused and threatened cancellation, but on discovering that no other firm was willing to supply these engines for less than £2,450 each they agreed provided all six were delivered before the end of July 1878. Assembly by

Neilson then proceeded apace with the first, No 33, reaching Highbridge on 24 June 1878 and Nos 34 to 38 during the following month.

The cylinders, motion, wheels, boiler and other features were similar to those of the 1874–6 Midland 4ft 6in 0-6-0 tanks while the tenders followed those supplied to the earlier Johnson Derby-built engines, although a narrowing of the water tanks enabled the springs to be sited above the running plate. They were appreciably smaller than any of the Johnson designs of Midland 0-6-0, the boiler barrel being 6in, the firebox 11in and the wheelbase 1ft 6in less. Nevertheless, they were instantly recognisable as being the work of Johnson and constructed under the auspices of Derby drawing office. The dimensions were as follows:

Cylinders	17in × 24in
Coupled wheels	4ft 6in
Wheelbase	7ft 4in + 7ft 8in = 15ft 0in
Boiler diameter	4ft 2in
Boiler length	10ft 0in
Firebox length	5ft 0in
Boiler pitch	6ft 9in
Heating surfaces:	*sq ft*
Tubes (215 × 1¾in)	1,033
Firebox	91
Total	1,124
Working pressure	140lb
Grate area	15sq ft
Weight in working order:	*tons cwt*
Leading coupled wheels	12 5
Centre coupled wheels	11 15
Trailing coupled wheels	9 19
Engine total	33 19
Tender (2,200gal)	28 12
Engine and tender	62 11

The chimney, dome and safety valve casings, and cab were typically Johnson, though the dome was 2in lower than those of the Avonside bogie tanks. Therefore these goods were the first Derby-designed engines to carry the shortened dome casing which brought the spring balances lower and gave the better known Johnson dome casing as distinct from that having an attenuated waist below the decorative top which hitherto had appeared on all that engineer's engines. The boiler differed from that of the 1874–6 tanks by having 215 instead of 220 $1\frac{3}{4}$in tubes, the reduction being caused by a rearrangement of the tube layout to gain increased clearance at the bottom of the barrel. Braking was by steam on both the engine and tender. Cast-iron shoes were fitted to the front of all coupled wheels with two-plate pattern hangers and outside pull rods. Later vacuum ejectors were added for train control and these operated the steam braking of the engine and tender wheels. Compared with the Fowlers these 0-6-0s were less powerful, not only as regards rated tractive force, but also by having smaller fire-boxes. Notwithstanding they supplanted this class on the heaviest freight duties over the Bath Extension and for over twenty years gave an excellent account of themselves. The boiler steamed more freely than that of the Fowlers while the braking was much more positive, a great asset on engines habitually engaged hauling unbraked goods trains over a steeply graded line. The men always referred to them, and the later Vulcan Foundry series, as the 'Scotties' because of their Scottish origin and this designation was adopted officially by both Highbridge and Derby Works.

Nos 33 to 38 had only been in service a few months when tenders were sought for another six. These were considered on 20 March 1879 when the Vulcan Foundry's offer of £2,090 each was accepted with delivery scheduled for the end of the year. Once again difficulties were encountered by the makers who wrote suggesting a reduction of £45 per engine if their completion was delayed six months, but the directors threatened cancellation which apparently had the desired effect, for as Nos 39 to 44 they reached Highbridge between 5 December

1879 and 19 December following. In general terms their design was similar to the earlier series, although whereas they were based on the Midland's 1874 0-6-0 tanks, the Vulcans were tender editions of the 1878 tanks—thus there were differences of which the most important concerned the shape of the inner firebox and the motion. The reversing lever rotated through 33° as against 38½° on the earlier series which had the reversing-shaft 2in and the reversing-rod 4in higher. This feature made Nos 33 to 38 readily distinguishable when viewed from the right, since like the Midland the Somerset & Dorset drove from that side.

The adoption of 2¾in tyres led to the coupled wheels becoming 4ft 6½in on tread while the tenders differed by having less highly arched frame-spaces between the horn-plates as well as oval spaces ahead of the leading horn-plates. The changed dimensions were as follows:

Heating surfaces:	*sq ft*	
Tubes (215 × 1¾in)	1,029	
Firebox	98	
Total	1,127	
Grate area	14¾sq ft	
Weight in working order:	*tons*	*cwt*
Leading coupled wheels	11	12
Centre coupled wheels	13	16
Trailing coupled wheels	9	2
Engine total	34	10
Tender	29	10
Engine and tender	64	0

According to the Midland drawings the tenders held 3 tons of coal and 2,040gal of water as against the 2 tons and 2,200gal of Nos 33 to 38, but later all twelve tenders were quoted at 3 tons and 2,200gal. New tender tanks were fitted about the time of reboilering when it appears the opportunity was taken to standardise the capacity.

Further batches of similar engines from the Vulcan Foundry were introduced between 1881 and 1890, their details being as follows:

Date ordered	Cost (£)	Maker's Nos	S & DJR Nos	Dates delivered
18 March 1880	2,340	896 to 899	25 to 28	July to August 1881
4 April 1883	2,475	1055 to 1060	46 to 51	August to September 1884
9 May 1889	2,180	1264 to 1269	56 to 61	June to July 1890

When all were in traffic there was a total of twenty-eight, all known as the Scotties after the 1878 Neilson batch. Nos 56 to 61 were delivered fitted with vacuum ejectors to enable use to be made of them on passenger trains when necessary while on 6 August 1890 authorisation was given to similarly equip the remainder of the class at an estimated cost of £50 per engine and tender. The steam brake was retained but henceforth was controlled by the vacuum system.

On a line possessing the sharp grades and long single sections of the Somerset & Dorset it was essential not to overload engines so a carefully calculated table showing the maximum

Number of wagons	Bath–Evercreech Junction						Evercreech Junction–Wimborne		
	Banked			Unaided					
	Goods	Coal	Empty	Goods	Coal	Empty	Goods	Coal	Empty
Class									
Fox, Walker 0-6-0ST	28	23	40	16	13	25	38	30	49
Fowler goods	26	22	37	15	12	23	35	27	45
Scottie goods	26	22	37	15	12	23	35	27	45
Bogie tanks	20	16	28	14	10	18	28	20	35
2-4-0									
Nos 17 & 18	Use	prohi	bited o	ver thi	s sectio	n	25	20	33
Nos 25A to 28A	,,	,,	,,	,,	,,		15	10	20

loadings was included in the working timetables and in practice rigidly enforced. Details are as shown on the previous page.

All loads were exclusive of brake vans, of which two had to be coupled to the rear of all goods, cattle and mineral trains passing over the Bath–Evercreech Junction section of the line. In bad weather loads could be decreased if absolutely necessary while for calculating purposes three empty wagons were the equal of two loaded ones. No train was to exceed fifty vehicles between Burnham and Wimborne or forty between Bath and Evercreech Junction.

It will be noted that the Fox, Walker saddle tanks were still the most powerful engines on the line and until 1890 regularly took a turn with the main line goods services despite their restricted supplies of coal and water. Use was also made of the bogie tanks for the shorter distance and lighter services until the turn of the century while the elderly England 2-4-os Nos 17 and 18 were restricted to the easier sections of the line. Over the years the Scotties were involved in several accidents, some serious and others quite trivial. The first worthy of mention occurred on 10 May 1883 when No 36 was propelling some loaded coal wagons in the sidings at Highbridge and the resident locomotive superintendent, B. S. Fisher, was crossing the tracks en route to the works. He absent mindedly passed between two rakes of wagons and was crushed to death by those being shunted by No 36. On being appointed in his stead, W. H. French immediately forbade all such shunting by tender engines and had stretches of fencing erected at dangerous points in the yards. The same engine was again in trouble on 11 November 1885 when it was derailed on leaving the shed roads by a shunter attempting to alter the points, while on 3 February 1886 it was in collision at Binegar with bogie tank No 53 and an up goods which had overrun signals in dense fog. No 36, banked by Fox, Walker saddle tank No 9, was at the head of the 1.30am down goods ex-Bath and was scheduled to wait at Binegar for an up train, but by oversight the driver passed through the station at speed to crash into No 53 just clear of the loop points. Damage was extensive and the fireman of the up train was killed.

In the previous year No 53 on 31 July had again been in collision at Binegar, on that occasion Scottie No 48 was the unfortunate co-participant. This accident occurred on the morning that the second line was opened to Chilcompton and while the locking-bars had been removed from the signal cabin for modification. Therefore the safety of all trains rested on the signalman's memory and his manipulation of the points and signals. Unfortunately, he turned the bogie tank and its train along the wrong track under clear signals with the result that it ran into No 48 standing on the down line in Binegar station causing severe damage and killing one passenger and the passenger guard. At the time the Board of Trade inspector was inspecting the new line, so he had an excellent view of the affray.

The next accident happened on 5 February 1895 after No 46 had banked the 12.45am Bath–Templecombe goods to Masbury and was returning light engine to Radstock. The crew maintained such a poor look-out that they passed signals at danger approaching Binegar and collided with the rear of the 12.10am Templecombe–Bath goods headed by Fowlers Nos 20 and 23. No 46's tender was badly crushed and derailed as were seven wagons of the goods while its crew and the goods guard were injured, the latter so severely that he never worked again.

For much of the year the line worked well below capacity, but during the summer months, and especially at weekends, the resources were regularly stretched to the limit with both engines and men having to work very long hours. Such a day was 10 July 1894, for no less than nine excursions were run from various Midland stations to Bournemouth and Poole while two more came from the Great Western. In the evening some time was lost getting so many trains away, but otherwise all went well until the last one destined for Worcester reached Templecombe where it was struck a glancing blow by Scottie No 57. This engine had worked a goods down from Bridgwater and after depositing the wagons it had shunted in the Upper Yard for about half an hour and was ready to transfer fourteen wagons to the Lower Yard as the Worcester excursion was signalled. The driver for some reason started away without looking at the signals and ran some 450yd before crashing into the side of the excursion's Pullman car and then scraping along the following seven carriages and the brake van. Damage mainly consisted of broken windows, torn off doors and foot-boarding and ripped panelling. Surprisingly no one was seriously injured. The excursion was double headed by Scottie No 46 and Fowler No 24, but as they had passed the point of impact both escaped unscathed although the couplings to the leading carriage were broken. At the inquiry Driver West of No 57 insisted that the signals were pulled off for him to proceed to the Lower Yard, but the Board of Trade reporting office refused to accept this as true and blamed him for the occurrence.

These summer excursions were undoubtedly financially viable, but they also created other problems not always appertaining to the provision of suitable motive power. For example, on 26 July 1901 Scotties Nos 35 and 47 were rostered for a sixteen-coach special from Gloucester to Bournemouth. The outward journey from Bath was uneventful, apart from the loss of 43 minutes, but the late evening return working spread chaos throughout the line for after preparing their engines both crews set out to view the sea and otherwise amuse themselves until duty called again. No 47's crew duly signed on and by 8.15pm were ready to leave the shed. Of the other crew there was no sign. Eventually they appeared showing all the signs of over indulgence at some hostelry en route from the sea front with the result that the foreman refused to let them take their engine out. As no spare men were to hand No 47 had to take the excursion alone and because of this 93 minutes were lost to Bath together with all the ensuing delays to other services on the way.

During the 1890s No 28 ran with a tender having a peculiarly curved weatherboard with two look-out windows which had been fashioned from the cab front of England 2-4-0 tank No 26A. Just why this odd fitting was added is not known, but it must have been of doubtful value when the engine was running chimney foremost since it acted as a scoop and cast a fierce blast of air across the footplate. Running tender first, however, the cab must have been extremely cosy. Possibly at this period No 28 was engaged on branch work.

The Scotties gave excellent service over the main line until 1894–5 when piloting of the heavier goods services became regular practice, especially in the winter months if the weather was bad. To avoid this it was decided on 6 February 1895 to obtain prices from Derby and Nine Elms Works for the construction of five of the more powerful Johnson 5ft 3in 0-6-0s. The two offers were considered on 8 May 1895 when that by the Midland Railway was accepted because of the lower cost and the promise of quicker delivery, details being as follows:

Derby   £1,960 each or £2,245 with manufacturer's profit added.

Nine Elms £1,980 each or £2,270 with manufacturer's profit added.

As Nos 62 to 66 these five engines reached the Somerset & Dorset between January and March 1896. The dimensions were as follows:

Cylinders	18in × 26in
Coupled wheels	5ft 2½in
Wheelbase	8ft 0in + 8ft 6in = 16ft 6in
Boiler diameter	4ft 2in
Boiler length	10ft 6in
Firebox length	5ft 11in
Boiler pitch	7ft 2in
Heating surfaces:	*sq ft*
Tubes (244 × 1⅝in)	1,141
Firebox	110
Total	1,251
Grate area	17½sq ft
Working pressure	150lb
Weight in working order:	*tons cwt*
Leading coupled wheels	12 7
Centre coupled wheels	15 3

Trailing coupled wheels	11	1
Engine total	38	11
Tender	32	15
Engine and tender	71	6

Unlike the earlier 0-6-0s designed for the line by Johnson they were identical in every way, apart from the Highbridge vacuum ejector layout, with the Midland Railway's standard goods of 1890–5. Similarly the tenders followed Midland practice although only carrying 2,950gal of water and 3½ tons of coal. The springs were outside and below the running-plate while coal rails were fitted.

Like their Midland counterparts many constructional features followed those of the 4ft 6in 0-6-0s, the boiler barrel again being in three rings with the dome sited centrally while the firebox shell was round topped and flush with the barrel. A pair of spring balances were mounted on the dome and a lock-up safety valve over the firebox in a brass casing. Sanding was by steam to the front and rear of the driving wheels. The vacuum brake was provided for use with passenger stock and this controlled the steam system of the engine and tender. The steam cylinder was mounted horizontally and the ejectors followed previous Joint practice by being in the cab and using the right side handrailing as the brake pipe, an arrangement which was employed on the line even for engines built at Derby until 1902.

In traffic they had a distinct advantage over the earlier class and quickly gained an enviable reputation for hard work and reliability, and in consequence became known as the Bulldogs— a soubriquet they retained until scrapped. Like so many Johnson boilers, theirs was free steaming and easy on fuel while when employed on the main line passenger services in the summer months they showed a surprisingly good turn of speed. The larger wheels, lengthened firebox and higher boiler pressure made them the best mixed traffic engines yet to work on the line.

By 1900 goods traffic over the main line necessitated the provision of eighteen through and seven pick-up trains in either direction while others had to be made available as required for the Binegar stone traffic and cattle specials. So once again more goods engines were necessary, but when Whitaker requested five additional Bulldogs on 7 August 1901 a decision was deferred for a year. Authorisation was finally granted on 6 August 1902 and as the need was now most urgent Derby agreed that the last five of sixty M class o-6-os ordered at £3,185 each from Neilson, Reid & Co in October 1900 should be diverted to the Somerset & Dorset, and as Nos 72 to 76 they duly arrived in September 1902. It has been suggested that they were destined to become Nos 69 to 73, but this must be incorrect since the letter dispatched to the makers notifying them of their changed destination clearly stated Nos 72 to 76. They entered service painted Midland red with their tenders lettered SDJR in the standard Highbridge fashion, but the buffer-beam lettering was in Derby's block style. They differed from the earlier series by having deeper frames which stood above the running plate to the rear of the smokebox, larger 3,250gal tenders, a 160lb working pressure and a greater weight. The ejector arrangements followed Derby practice, apart from the provision of an independent blower, the valve of which was sited outside the smokebox on the left side with the cab operating rod running below the boiler barrel handrailing. On the Midland at this period it was not customary to fit an independent blower on vacuum-equipped engines, it being standard practice to use the ejector exhaust to create the necessary draught. The weight in working order was as follows:

	tons	cwt
Leading wheels	13	0
Driving wheels	14	19
Trailing wheels	11	16
Engine total	39	15
Tender	37	0
Engine and tender	76	15

Thicker tyres increased the coupled wheel diameter to 5ft 3in.

These engines, and Nos 62 and 66, were subsequently fitted with extra sandboxes, hand operated, below the running plate which delivered sand to the front of the leading coupled wheels. At the same time the sandboxes ahead of the centre coupled wheels were also converted from steam to gravity feed, but for some reason steam was retained for the boxes serving the rear side of these wheels until after reboilering. Other late changes included the use of Deeley parallel-sided chimneys with capuchons and smokebox doors secured by clips and bolts. No 74 carried such a door before reboilering while still fitted with an original Johnson pattern chimney. In contrast No 72 was running at the same time with a Deeley chimney and a Johnson smokebox door.

Returning to the Scottie goods reboilering became necessary in May 1889 when No 35 was fitted with a Johnson replacement boiler of similar pattern and size to that discarded, except that the distance between the tubeplates was slightly greater. Dates of the other reboilerings were: 1889: No 36 (October); 1890: Nos 33 (December), 40 (January), 42 (June), 44 (August); 1891: Nos 28 (November), 34 (March), 43 (July); 1892: No 27 (May); 1893: No 37 (April); 1896: Nos 39 (January), 41 (February); 1897: Nos 26 (January), 38 (March); 1900: No 47 (November); 1901: No 50 (April); 1903: Nos 25 (September), 46 (February), 48 (May), 49 (November), 51 (January). Nine engines later received a second new boiler of this type, these being: 1898: Nos 36 (November), 40 (April), 42 (October); 1899: No 27 (July); 1900: No 28 (January); 1901: No 43 (October); 1902: No 44 (October); 1903: Nos 35, 37 (June). Some of these boilers were probably second-hand with new fireboxes and tubes, the repairs being undertaken at Derby. Before 1896 iron was used for the construction of new boilers, but thereafter steel was employed. Some engines (eg No 37) received full-length Midland chimneys while others (eg No 43) were given a later pattern cast-iron chimney of larger diameter but of less height. Later parallel-sided Deeley chimneys with capuchons were also used while in LMS days No 42 ran with a Deeley chimney of the tall variety found on the Joint bogie tanks.

Of the 1890 batch Nos 58, 59 and 61 received a second-hand Johnson replacement boiler in March 1889, January 1900 and September 1898 respectively. Otherwise it was 1906 before re-boilering commenced with a modified version of the original Johnson design with that engineer's final arrangement of boiler mountings (ie closed domes and Ramsbottom safety valves and a lock-up valve over the firebox) and Deeley's arrangement of tubes in vertical rows. The heating surfaces were tubes (196 × 1¾in) 932sq ft and firebox 91sq ft. The grate area was 14·6sq ft and the working pressure 160lb. Dates were as follows: 1906: Nos 56 (October), 57 (November); 1907: No 59 (July); 1908: Nos 60 (May), 61 (September); 1909: No 58 (January).

In 1908 similar Johnson–Deeley pattern boilers were provided for four of the 1879–81 series, these being Nos 26 (November), 28 (July), 40 (September) and 44 (December). The last mentioned, however, only retained its new boiler for five years when it was replaced in January 1914 by the Johnson pattern left spare by the scrapping of Vulcan Foundry 2-4-0 No 15A. A similar boiler ex-No 16A was fitted to No 37 in the same month.

Withdrawal commenced in October 1914 with Nos 27, 33, 34 and 43, all having spent some months laid aside before being officially written off. For goods engines the final mileages were most creditable, although only No 34 with 1,019,438 topped the million mark. No others were condemned before 1922 when Nos 35 to 39 were replaced by the much larger Class 4s Nos 57 to 61. The arrival of the latter necessitated some renumbering of the remaining Scotties and since the 1878 Neilson series had all been discarded, Nos 56 to 61 were changed to 33 to 38. For a time, to permit the men to become accustomed to this, they ran with both old and new numbers.

Further withdrawals occurred in 1925 when Nos 41, 46, 48 and 51 were dispensed with while in 1928 these were followed by Nos 25, 26, 28 and 33 (ex-No 57). This left only eleven in traffic and as much happened at the time to confuse identities they are best dealt with under three separate headings.

Taking the five remaining 1890 engines first, these were rebuilt at Highbridge in 1927–9 with very deep, substantial frames and new cylinders, and 160lb G5 Midland boilers having Belpaire fireboxes and Ross pop safety valves. New spectacle plates were provided, but otherwise the original cabs were re-used. The dates were as follows: 1927: No 37 (November); 1929: Nos 34 (December), 36 (May), 38 (March); 1929: No 35 (March). At the same time the tenders from withdrawn 4-4-0s Nos 15 and 16 were attached to Nos 34 and 35, these weighing 32 tons 18cwt and carrying 2,600gal. The changed heating surfaces and working order weights were as follows:

	sq ft	
Tubes (194 × 1¾in)	923	
Firebox	85	
Total	1,008	
Grate area	14½sq ft	
	tons	cwt
Leading wheels	11	13
Driving wheels	14	8
Trailing wheels	10	6
Engine total	36	7

Nos 40, 42, 44, 47 and 49 were renumbered 67 to 71 in August 1928 while on the same date No 50 for not quite the same readily apparent reason became 51. These engines can be divided into two groups according to the boilers carried: (1) Nos 69 and 71: Deeley pattern with closed dome and firebox Ramsbottom safety valves in a large casing, these boilers being obtained second-hand in May 1929 and November 1928 respectively from Nos 35 and 33 when they were rebuilt with Belpaire G5 boilers. (2) Nos 51, 67, 68 and 70: Johnson pattern with spring-balance safety valves on the dome and a lock-up valve in a brass casing over the firebox. Of these the last two had carried these boilers since 1899–1900, but No 51 had received its boiler from No 25 in January 1929 and No 67 from No 29 in June 1925, although previously it carried a Deeley pattern fitted in 1908. Thus the eleven survivors on 31 December 1929 carried no less than three different types of boiler; nevertheless, all were classified 1F by the LMS who allotted Nos 2880 to 2890 (ex-Nos 34 to 38, 51, 67 to 71). Within a few months Nos 2886 and 2888 had been withdrawn and replaced by Kirtley double-framed 0-6-0s Nos 2687 and 2817, but Nos 2889 and 2890 were found regular employment on the Burnham branch and other light duties until November 1932. No 2887 travelled quite widely in the autumn of 1930, it being noted on vans at Bournemouth, shunting at Bath and on a local goods at Saltley within a matter of weeks.

Despite their extensive 1927–9 rebuilding Belpaire boilered Nos 2880 to 2884 only just outlasted those not so favoured for all were condemned in December 1932. Class 3F 0-6-0s took their place on the Burnham branch and elsewhere. The final mileages were high for goods engines, ranging from 744,819 by No 43 to 1,023,133 by No 40 (2886).

At the turn of the century the Bulldogs were well on top of their daily tasks, but by 1907 there was a demand for more powerful engines and in March 1907 Derby offered the choice of two outside cylinder 0-8-0 designs. Unfortunately, neither could be accommodated by the bridges and it was 1914 before the more acceptable 2-8-0s were to hand and could relieve the now outclassed 0-6-0s on the hardest main line duties. Needless to say there remained numerous lighter tasks suitable for Bulldog operation, so when 4-4-0s Nos 70 and 71 were broken up in 1914 their comparatively new H-type boilers were repaired and made available for further employment. Similar boilers had been used extensively by the Midland to reboiler the Johnson 5ft 3in six-coupled goods, so Highbridge took advantage of these spares to convert Nos 63 and 66 into the most powerful 0-6-0s on the line, details being: No 63 (October 1914), boiler from No 70 (new November 1903); No 66 (April 1914), boiler from No 71 (new November 1903).

At Derby such reboilering often involved a lengthening of the frames by 13in at the rear and the provision of a new cab, but for Nos 63 and 66 new frames were supplied, these being deeper than the originals and having straight tops ahead of the smoke-box. The cabs off the scrapped 4-4-0s were re-used after the roofs had been extended, pillar supports added and the side-sheets modified to give rectangular splashers for the trailing wheels. The chimney was a queer mixture of Deeley and Johnson practice, it being basically a Johnson flowerpot with a Deeley capuchon. The weight in working order was increased to:

		tons	cwt
Leading wheels		14	10
Driving wheels		15	15
Trailing wheels		14	6
Total		44	11

Boiler diameter	4ft 8in
Boiler length	10ft 5$\frac{15}{16}$in
Firebox length	7ft 0in
Boiler pitch	7ft 8in

	No 63	No 66
Tubes	239 × 1$\frac{3}{4}$in	242 × 1$\frac{3}{4}$in
Heating surfaces:	sq ft	sq ft
Tubes	1,207	1,222
Firebox	125	125
Total	1,332	1,347

Grate area	21sq ft
Working pressure	175lb

Because of their large boilers and six-coupled wheels these two engines were frequently rostered for main line passenger service between 1914 and 1920. This was particularly noticeable from the mileage returns of 1915–18, details being as follows:

Engine No	Mileage at reboilering	Mileage at 31 December 1918	Average yearly mileage
No 63	438,124	559,670	30,389
No 66	395,098	521,302	31,551

Their success would probably have led to others of the class being similarly rebuilt but for World War I when shortages of manpower and materials necessitated many old and practically worn-out boilers and fireboxes being patched up for another spell of duty. After hostilities ceased the G7 Belpaire version of the H1 boiler came into general use and in course of time was fitted to all ten engines. In all essential particulars, apart from the firebox, the G7 boiler followed the superseded pattern so the grate area and working pressure were unchanged while the heating surfaces were only marginally altered. Details of the latter were:

	sq ft
Tubes (252 × 1¾in)	1,257
Firebox	123
Total	1,380

Weight in working order:

	tons	cwt
Leading wheels	14	12
Driving wheels	16	2
Trailing wheels	14	14
Total	45	8

Dates of reboilering were: 1920: Nos 63 (September), 66 (May); 1921: Nos 64 (March), 65 (December); 1923: Nos 62 (May), 76 (November); 1924: Nos 73 (July), 74 (April), 75 (November); 1925: No 72 (October). All the material was supplied by Derby works and dispatched to Highbridge where the work was undertaken, the more important items being as follows: frames 1⅛in thick, frame stretchers for front of firebox,

3 right-hand, and 3 left-hand sandboxes, 1 set of manganese-bronze axleboxes, new cab, trailing splashers and toolbox, smokebox wrapper plate, smokebox door, chimney, blast pipe, pair of connecting rods with solid little ends and front end buffers. Nos 63 and 66 did not receive new frames according to the list of material dispatched from Derby, but a note in the Highbridge Register stated that two sets of frames (ex-Nos 63 and 66) were sent to Derby on 24 November 1920. Having received new and longer frames in 1914 to take the H boiler there was no need for renewal in 1920, but this appears to have occurred. Some years earlier, in May 1914, Nos 72 and 75 had lost their 3,250gal tenders to superheater 4-4-0s Nos 70 and 71, and in exchange received smaller 2,950gal tenders from withdrawn large Johnson 4-4-0s Nos 70 and 71. Similarly early in 1921 Nos 73, 74 and 76 lost their original tenders to new superheater 4-4-0s Nos 67 to 69 and received in their place 2,950gal tenders from large Johnson 4-4-0 No 69 (withdrawn 1919) and Deeley 4-4-0s Nos 77 and 78. This brought the later series in line with Nos 62 to 66. The earlier rebuilds such as Nos 63, 64 and 66 came out of shops blue, but those dealt with later were black. Standard Midland vacuum ejector mountings appeared on Nos 62 to 66 around this period while later mechanical lubrication was provided for the axleboxes and the fitting of thicker tyres increased the wheel diameter to 5ft 3in. Apart from the sanding arrangements and mechanical lubricators these Highbridge G7 rebuilds bore a remarkable resemblance to the genuine Derby article and exhibited none of the vagaries which the Midland & Great Northern contrived to introduce with its Melton Constable G7 rebuilds of its Johnson 0-6-0s. In traffic the Midland rebuilds proved particularly free steaming and these were found equally capable and always gave a good account of themselves.

The arrival of the 2-8-0s and the Class 4 0-6-0s naturally reduced the need for their use on the main line goods services although they remained much in demand as pilots for the heavy summer holiday expresses and excursions. When taken into LMS stock they filled vacancies in the ex-Midland 0-6-0 series,

thus Nos 62 to 66 became Nos 3194, 3198, 3201, 3204 and 3211
while Nos 72 to 76 became Nos 3216, 3218, 3228, 3248 and
3260. As the small Johnson o-6-os were withdrawn so they took
over their duties including the Burnham branch. The allocation
in 1937 was: Templecombe: Nos 3194/9, 3201/4/11/28/60;
Bath: No 3248; Highbridge: Nos 3216/18. By this date all had
received exchange boilers following visits to Derby for overhaul
and this led to Ross pop safety valves replacing the Rams-
bottoms. Various tender changes also occurred, the replacements being of the Midland 3,250gal pattern.

All ten remained working on the Somerset & Dorset section,
in contrast to other Joint classes, until World War II when a
number were transferred away to various LMS sheds. Nonethe-
less, a fair proportion remained faithful so that at the end of
hostilities Templecombe had the services of Nos 3198, 3248 and
3260, Highbridge Nos 3194, 3216 and 3218, and Bath Nos
3204 and 3248 while No 3211 was at Toton and No 3201 at
Saltley. At nationalisation they entered British Railways, except
for No 3198 which had been condemned the previous month,
and were allotted numbers in the usual 40,000 series, although
No 3260 suffered a pitch-in and was broken up in 1949, before
the change occurred. No 43201 of Saltley returned home, but
No 43211 moved to Hasland and later to Trafford Park.

On 19 August 1949 No 3260 was heading the early morning
Templecombe–Bridgwater mixed train when a small petrol
engine owned by the Eclipse Peat Company was run into at
speed on the unprotected level crossing near Ashcott. It was
foggy and the crew failed to see the broken down engine until
too late so the impact was violent and No 3260 ploughed its
way into the adjacent South Drain from where salvage was only
possible by use of acetylene cutters, after the water had been
diverted.

The centenary of the Somerset Central Railway was in 1954,
and this was celebrated by running a special train between
Glastonbury and Burnham hauled by No 43201 suitably renumbered 64 and lettered SDJR. This train was organised by
Messrs C. & J. Clark of Street and Clark, Son & Morland of

Glastonbury, the shoe manufacturers, in which one of the chief promoters of the line, James Clark of Street, had been a partner. The twelve-coach train was filled to standing with descendants of this gentleman, the employees of the firms and their families, many being in period costume. No 64 gave of its best and the day was a great success.

Those remaining in traffic performed their normal round of duties for the next few years, but the end was fast approaching and by the end of 1959 only Nos 43194, 43216 and 43218 were still at work on the Somerset & Dorset and No 43211 at Trafford Park. Two of these went in 1960 and No 43211 in the following year which left No 43216 to struggle on alone until August 1962.

CHAPTER EIGHT

THE RADSTOCK SHUNTERS

One of the main objectives of the Bath Extension was to gain access to the collieries in the hills and valleys around Radstock. For centuries their output of coal had been carried by cart or packhorse, but in 1805 much of this was transferred to the Somersetshire Coal Canal which followed the Cam valley for ten miles from the Kennet & Avon at the Dundas aqueduct to a terminal basin between Timsbury and Paulton. From Midford a branch was planned to Radstock, but this was only partly constructed and in 1815 a horse tramway with branches to the outlying pits was laid along the abandoned towpath. By the middle of the century the Canal Company was the most prosperous in southern England and offered such an efficient, cheap and reliable means of transportation that the opening of the Frome to Radstock broad-gauge branch of the Wilts, Somerset & Weymouth Railway in November 1854 had little effect on the volume of traffic carried. The 1871 Act authorising the construction of the Bath Extension also permitted the purchase of the canal tramway and advantage was taken of this to follow its line for about six miles from Radstock to midway between Wellow and Midford when laying the standard-gauge track. Other tramways in the area were also acquired while a number of new connecting lines were put in by the Somerset & Dorset which not only had achieved its aim of reaching the coal field but also had gained virtual control of its output.

For a decade or so the Somerset & Dorset covered its motive power requirements by means of horses, but by May 1882 it was becoming increasingly apparent that greater economy and efficiency could be achieved by the introduction of small steam locomotives. Therefore Fisher was instructed by the committee to investigate the second-hand market and in the following October reported the purchase of a light 0-4-0 saddle tank at a cost of £385 from C. D. Philips of Newport. Named *Bristol* it had been supplied thirty years earlier by Slaughter, Gruning & Co to the Grays Chalk Quarries of Grays, Essex, where it had been employed until June 1866. Then, with two worn-out tank engines, it was sold for £488 to the well-known second-hand locomotive dealer I. W. Boulton of Ashton-under-Lyne. After heavy repairs it was hired out on a number of occasions to J. Aird & Co and was engaged on contracting in various parts of the country, including the London area, until early 1872 when the Widnes Alkali Co paid £9 weekly for its services over a period of months before making a purchase at £540. Just how long this new source of activity lasted is not known, although in May 1880 C. D. Philips was advertising it for sale at £400 without repairs or £775 in good working order. Apparently no firm offer was received before Fisher's inspection on 11 October 1882 and its acceptance by the Somerset & Dorset for £385 as it stood.

On inspection at Highbridge the boiler was found in such poor condition that it had to be condemned and a new one ordered. This became available in April 1883, but was not fitted until the end of the following month after the frames had been strengthened and the buffering gear modified to conform to main line standards. The dimensions were then as follows: cylinders (outside): 10in × 14in, wheels: 3ft, wheelbase: 6ft 0in, heating surfaces: 582sq ft, working pressure: 110lb, tank capacity: 383gal, and weight: 13¼ tons. To reduce the overall height the original chimney was removed and a short stove pipe fitted while the front spectacle plate was extended rearwards to give better footplate protection. The brass nameplates were attached to the saddle tank above the leading wheels. In the repair register recording was by name only until December 1891 when a red ink entry stated: 'altered from No 45 to 45A 15 November 1891.' It was the only engine owned by the

THE VULCAN FOUNDRY TANKS

Page 135 (*Top*) 0-4-4T No 53. As built in 1885. (*Bottom*) 0-4-4T No 55 as rebuilt in 1925 with Belpaire firebox and Fowler fittings. Note the modifications to the front look-out windows

THE SMALL 4-4-0s

Page 136 (*Top*) 4-4-0 No 15 as built in 1891. (*Middle*) 4-4-0 No 68 on the 1896 series, as rebuilt in 1908. (*Bottom*) 4-4-0 No 17 at Radstock in 1929. This photograph shows the locomotive as reboilered in 1927 and especially the modifications to the cab

Somerset & Dorset to carry a name and it is quite remarkable that after such diverse wanderings *Bristol* should end its working life so near the West Country seaport after which it had been named.

Not being intended for steam operation many of the spurs and sidings around Radstock were of light construction and sharp curvature, so it is not surprising that *Bristol* suffered a number of minor derailments and pitch-ins during its early years of service. Only one serious incident is on record, this occurring on 18 May 1884 when thirteen empty wagons were being propelled over the Tyning loop. In pouring rain the pointsman accidentally turned the slowly moving train over the wrong line and into a rake of loaded wagons in charge of two horses named Jeannie and Sarah. Both were killed and seven wagons badly battered by the impact, while *Bristol* escaped with sundry dents and abrasions. At the subsequent inquiry it was discovered that the crew of *Bristol* consisted of a 67-year-old driver and a lad of fourteen, the latter travelling on the buffers of the leading wagon ready to dismount as necessary to adjust points or to attend to the coupling and uncoupling of wagons. French, the resident locomotive superintendent, was severely censured for permitting such manning and was ordered to draw up a more stringent set of rules and to see that they were put into operation within 48 hours. At the same time £1,830 was authorised for setting up an elementary signalling system and relaying various sharp curves to make the colliery lines more suitable for steam power so that the employment of horses could be discontinued. This work was completed in June 1885 when a small 0-4-2 saddle tank was commenced at Highbridge Works. Numbered 25A it was completed at a cost of £895 in the following December, the dimensions being:

Cylinders (outside)	10in × 14in
Coupled wheels	3ft 6in
Trailing wheels	2ft 3in
Wheelbase	5ft 1in + 4ft 9in = 9ft 10in
Boiler diameter	2ft 7in

E

Boiler length	7ft 2in
Firebox length	2ft 3in
Boiler pitch	4ft 11½in

Heating surfaces:	sq ft
Tubes (53 × 1⅞in)	192
Firebox	29½
Total	221½

Working pressure	140lb
Grate area	4¼sq ft

Weight in working order:	tons	cwt
Leading wheels	6	7
Driving wheels	7	7
Trailing wheels	3	9
Total	17	3

Water capacity	370gal

The straight-topped boiler had a small dome with attached spring-balance safety valves over the firebox, a copper-capped chimney, and was fed by an injector and a pump driven by the left-hand cross-head. The square cab enclosed the small bunker which must have made coaling a tedious and all-embracing task. The saddle tank extended from the rear of the smokebox to the front of the firebox with the filler cap close to the leading end. The springs of the coupled axles were above the running-plate, but those of the trailing axle were in slots cut in the frames beneath the footplate and under the cab where they must have been practically inaccessible. The wheels were of forged-steel without balance weights and the braking was by steam via cast-iron shoes and double-plate hangers to the front of the coupled wheels. The sanding layout was unusual for there were large containers on either side for backward running yet only a diminutive sandbox on the right side for forward working. It was many years before a more balanced arrangement was fitted.

The duties at Radstock were both numerous and various, and

must have kept this engine and *Bristol* fully extended, since, in addition to the yards, there was the short branch to Middle Pit and the foot of the Clandown incline, the spur to Ludlow and, a mile nearer Bath at Writhlington box, the Braysdown sidings serving an incline and the siding to Writhlington pit-head.

Bristol received its last heavy repairs in March 1892 and when laid aside unserviceable in April 1895 was replaced by No 45A, a neat four-coupled saddle tank recently completed at a cost of £1,095 by Highbridge Works. A second, and similar engine, numbered 26A, entered traffic in the following October. The overall height of these engines like that of their predecessors was severely restricted by the extremely low arch of Tyning Bridge under which they had to pass to reach the Great Western sidings.

The saddle tank extended to the front of the smokebox while the coal was contained in deep 'fenders' either side of the firebox. All the springs were above the axleboxes, the cylinders steeply inclined, the crossheads of the one-bar variety, the big ends of the closed type with wedge-block and vertical screw and the little-ends bushed, while the coupling rods had plain bushed ends. The boiler was flush topped with a tall dome and attached spring-balance safety valves over the firebox. Braking was by steam and sanding by gravity to the front and rear of the driving wheels. When new No 45A had an open footplate, but before No 26A entered traffic an all-over single-plate cab was fitted to give nominal protection to the crew. The latter was always so equipped. The dimensions were as follows:

Cylinders (outside)	10in × 14in
Coupled wheels	3ft 0in
Wheelbase	6ft 0in
Boiler diameter	2ft 7in
Boiler length	8ft 2in
Firebox length	1ft 9½in
Boiler pitch	4ft 11in
Heating surfaces:	*sq ft*
Tubes (69 × 1¾in)	273

Firebox	37
Total	310

Working pressure	150lb
Grate area	5sq ft

Weight in working order:	tons	cwt
Leading wheels	8	4
Trailing wheels	11	4
Total	19	8

Weight empty	16 tons 8cwt
Water capacity	500gal
Coal capacity	5cwt

Despite their mundane duties far away from the public eye all the Radstock shunters were painted in the full passenger blue livery and were always so well polished by their crews that they became known as the 'Dazzlers'—a nickname they retained to the end notwithstanding the use of plain black in later years.

In April 1896 No 25A was involved in an accident near the foot of the Clandown incline; no one was injured but the damage sustained was sufficient for a visit being made to Highbridge where the boiler was condemned and replaced by one similar to those carried by the two 1895 engines. At the same time the saddle tank was extended to the front of the smokebox and a taller chimney, still of the built-up pattern with a polished cap, fitted, while the elaborate cab was discarded in favour of a simple, single-plate type leaving the bunker open for coaling. The firebox dome was taller with the safety-valve levers to the front instead of passing through into the cab, and the pump on the left side was discarded in favour of two injectors under the wings of the saddle tank. Changes were also made to the brake-gear, the blocks on single-plate hangers being placed between the two pairs of coupled wheels. Deeper wooden buffer beams were raised slightly above the level of the running plate. When

returned to traffic in October 1896 the changed dimensions
were as follows:

Boiler diameter	2ft 7in
Boiler length	7ft 5in
Firebox length	1ft 9½in
Heating surfaces:	*sq ft*
Tubes (69 × 1¾in)	250
Firebox	37
Total	287
Grate area	5sq ft
Working pressure	150lb

Weight in working order:	*tons*	*cwt*
Leading wheels	8	2
Driving wheels	8	11
Trailing wheels	4	0
Total	20	13

Empty weight	17 tons 10cwt
Tank capacity	430gal

Part of the coal was carried in 'fenders' alongside the firebox
on either side of the engine. This increased the capacity to 8cwt,
although a more inaccessible position would have been difficult
to devise.

Heavy repairs again became necessary in October 1906 when
11in cylinders were fitted and the vacuum brake added so that
it could be used on the Highbridge–Burnham workmen's trains
and also as the works pilot. It was not a success and with the
vacuum equipment removed was returned to Radstock to re-
join Nos 26A and 45A. All three remained there until the
autumn of 1918 when No 26A was hired by the War Department and for several months worked on Poole Quay before
going to the Holton Heath Cordite Factory. A photograph
appeared in one of the local papers showing it in the back-
ground when a new fire appliance was officially handed over,
the tallish chimney having been replaced by a shortened version

topped by a spark arrester. On return to Radstock the original chimney may have been refitted, but if so the lower pattern plus spark arrester was in use again by 1926.

By mid-1928 the boilers were showing signs of their age and it became necessary to consider either reboilering or withdrawal and replacement by other suitable small engines. At first it was decided to replace them by three ex-Lancashire & Yorkshire 0-4-0 tanks, but as these required a crew of two no saving in running costs could be expected and the idea was discarded in favour of two 200hp double-engined and geared Sentinel shunters at a cost of £1,950 each. Being single-manned they could be expected to cost £354 less per annum than a conventional steam locomotive, the respective costs being £715 and £1,069. These figures obviously included fuel, oil and maintenance as well as wages. Delivery was made in February and May 1929, when they took over the Ludlow, Writhlington and Clandown colliery duties, and also various shunting duties at Radstock.

The three Dazzlers were officially laid aside in February 1929, but Nos 26A and 45A were both in steam and at work during April, while No 45A assisted the first Sentinel until its partner arrived the following month. Thereafter No 26A was steamed at irregular intervals until the end of the year, when the LMS erroneously allotted it No 1509. It was eventually removed from stock in December 1930. No 25A latterly carried cast-iron wheels of 'box' pattern with 'H' section spokes and a shortened chimney topped by a spark arrester. Numbered 101 and 102, and painted black, the two Sentinels had the following dimensions:

Cylinders (4)	6¾in × 9in
Driving wheels	3ft 2in
Wheelbase	5ft 6in
Heating surfaces:	*sq ft*
Water tubes	108
Furnace walls	51
Total evaporative	159

Superheater	43	
Combined total	202	
Working pressure	275lb	
Coal	10cwt	
Water	600gal	
Weight in working order:	*tons*	*cwt*
Leading wheels	12	16
Trailing wheels	14	19
Total	27	15

They were powerful examples of their type and proved worthy substitutes for the three Dazzlers, although possibly never gaining the same popularity. All the bearings were outside, the axles being retained correctly positioned in relation to the driving chains by radius-rods connected to the axleboxes. At the leading end a pair of 100hp high-speed vertical enclosed Sentinel engines each with two cylinders drove on to a single reduction gear below them, from which the power was conducted by two chains inside the wheels to the axle of the leading wheels, with another coupling chain connected thence to the trailing pair. Lubrication of the cylinders and valve gear was by means of a force-feed pump driven by the crankshaft.

Steam was produced in a standard Sentinel water tube boiler with side firing while a superheater above the tubes gave a steam temperature of 500 to 600° F at full output. The exhaust from the engines passed through this superheater coil before discharging to the atmosphere via the four blast nozzles of the rectangular chimney on the cab roof. In summer the men often found the cab unbearably hot, much more so than a conventional shunter, although in winter it could be most comfortable. A 600gal water tank occupied the whole middle space between the engine and the boiler. The squat appearance and the general packing-in of parts was caused by the combined operating requirements of passage over sharp curves and the 10ft 5in Tyning Bridge.

In practice the anticipated economies of new motive power are seldom wholly realised, but these engines greatly exceeded all predictions. For the yearly costs of No 101 during the period January 1930 to December 1934 were £643, £705, £684, £587 and £698 respectively—an average of £643 per annum which was some 10 per cent better than envisaged. The figures for No 102 were not quite so good, although still below £715.

They became Nos 7190/1 when taken into LMS stock and at nationalisation Nos 47190/1, the livery being plain black. Apart from periodic visits to works for overhaul both spent practically their entire working life at Radstock. When both were out of service in 1931 their place was temporarily filled by ex-Lancashire & Yorkshire 0-4-0 tank No 11202. From time to time in later years similar engines had to be borrowed to cover routine repairs, these including No 11212 in July 1946, and No 51202 in June 1949 and again in March 1951.

In later years as the coal traffic dwindled one was sometimes employed by the ex-LMS running shed at Bristol from where No 47191 was condemned in August 1959. Its companion followed in March 1961 with a mileage of 291,073.

CHAPTER NINE

THE GOODS LOCOMOTIVES AND
SERVICES, 1906 to 1930

Goods and mineral traffic over the main line continued to increase yearly until 1906 when there was a rapid expansion following the Midland and South Western companies' decision to route as much of their own traffic as possible over the Somerset & Dorset. For instance the South Western drastically curtailed the goods traffic offered to the Great Western at Basingstoke, Salisbury and Exeter while the Midland made use of the line for much of its north-to-south freight which previously had travelled via London. Night traffic, therefore, became much heavier with no less than ten up trains being scheduled to depart from Templecombe between the hours of 10pm and 5am while it was necessary to provide twenty-one services daily from Bath, together with five coal and mineral trains from Radstock, Binegar or Winsor Hill. Cattle specials, too, were on the increase with no less than sixteen having to be laid on during October 1906. The yards at Evercreech were in use twenty-four hours a day with seldom more than a few brief slack periods in between trains.

Under these circumstances it is not surprising to find references in the minute books of Whitaker advocating the provision of additional and more powerful goods engines. Less expected is the discovery in January 1907 of Derby offering the choice of two 0-8-0 designs, one having 20in × 28in outside cylinders and a weight of 61½ tons and the other having 19½in × 26in outside cylinders and a weight of 59½ tons. Both incorporated a full range of standard Midland details, including undersized axleboxes and 3,500gal tenders. Whitaker would have happily accepted either design, although preferring the larger to give a reserve of power for future expansion of traffic, but the South Western's civil engineer refused to consider eight-coupled engines unless £34,700 was spent strengthening bridges, relaying track and lengthening sidings to accommodate the longer trains. The new 50ft turntable installed at a cost of £2,047 at Evercreech Junction three years ago would also be inadequate to take such large engines. Savings in operating costs were estimated at only £516 which was considered much too small a return for such a large outlay so the matter was deferred. All was not lost, however, for it was accepted that all future bridge and track renewing should be undertaken with the introduction of heavier locomotives in mind.

Whitaker, being near retirement, accepted the position and made the best of the resources available, but when M. F. Ryan succeeded him as resident locomotive superintendent on 24 July 1911 he had a fresh appraisal made of the project and discovered that a reduction of 6 tons in the weight carried by the coupled wheels would necessitate only £2,050 being spent by the civil engineer. The use of tender cabs would avoid the need of larger turntables since the engines could work equally well tender first at low speeds. Savings were estimated at £8,650 per annum by replacing eight old engines by six larger ones and increasing the size of the trains. These findings were acceptable to the civil engineer and authorisation was granted on 5 February 1913 for the construction of six such locomotives by Derby at a cost of £3,500 each. The weight reduction on the coupled wheels was achieved by adding a pony truck to the leading end and thereby obtaining a 2-8-0 which must have also improved the running and lessened the wear on the track. The first, No 80, arrived at Bath on 1 March 1914 and was immediately set to work on a series of test runs with heavy mineral trains over the line to Evercreech. These proved most successful and Nos 81 to 85 entered traffic during the next few months. The dimensions were as follows:

Cylinders	21in × 28in
Pony truck	3ft 3½in
Coupled wheels	4ft 7¾in
Wheelbase	8ft 3in + 6ft 0in +
	5ft 6in + 6ft 0in =
	25ft 9in
Boiler diameter	4ft 8in
Boiler length	11ft 11in
Firebox length	9ft 0in
Boiler pitch	8ft 10in
Heating surfaces:	*sq ft*
Tubes (148 × 1¾in +	
21 × 5⅛in)	1,182
Firebox	151
Total evaporative	1,333
Superheater	385sq ft
Working pressure	190lb
Grate area	28·4sq ft
Weight in working order:	*tons cwt*
Pony truck	8 15
Leading coupled	12 13
Intermediate coupled	13 16
Driving	15 16
Rear coupled	13 15
Total engine	64 15
Tender (3,500gal)	44 4
Total engine and tender	108 19

The boilers were of the Midland G9AS pattern as fitted to the superheated Midland Compound 4-4-0s and later to the standard LMS Compounds, although differing by having circular front tube-plates to suit the smokeboxes of the 2-8-0s. They were of the straight-topped Belpaire pattern, the barrel being in two rings with the dome on the rearmost and having a pair of Ramsbottom safety valves over the firebox with a separate auxiliary lock-up valve behind them. The superheater was a

Derby derivation of the Schmidt pattern with twenty-one flues set in three horizontal rows and having a steam-operated damper in the smokebox. This latter was of the drum pattern and was carried on a cast saddle. The firebox had an inclined grate similar to the superheated 4-4-0s while the ashpan was in two sections to clear the rear axle.

The outside cylinders were inclined at an angle of 1 in 12 to give clearance to platform faces and the Walschaerts valve gear was probably based on French and Italian drawings which Derby had 'borrowed'. Most of the motion for the valve gear was fluted as were the coupling and connecting rods. The return crank was fitted to the crank-pin using four studs in place of the more usual square end, a practice which was continued into LMS days and also appeared on various Ashford designs. The reversing gear was steam operated with its equipment mounted inside the main frames on the right-hand side. To allow for coasting down hills Fowler–Anderson by-pass valves were fitted. An eight-point mechanical lubricator supplied oil to the cylinders and valves.

A coupled wheelbase of 17ft 6in would appear to be too long for a route such as the Somerset & Dorset but nevertheless all the driving wheels were flanged and adequate control was provided by the pony truck. Springs for the coupled wheels were below the axleboxes with equalising beams between the front and intermediate and between the driving and rear while the pony truck springs were above the axleboxes. The brake gear received special attention and a total of three cylinders were used to give adequate power. Two of the cylinders were mounted under the rear drag-plates and worked in tandem to operate the brakes on the three rearward sets of coupled wheels. The third cylinder operated brakes on the front coupled wheels and clasp-type brakes on the pony truck. Vacuum equipment was also carried for use, when necessary, with passenger stock. Steam-operated sanding gear was provided for both forward and reverse running.

The tender was a standard Deeley design with the addition of a cab. It carried 7 tons of fuel and 3,500gal of water. No

turntables on the line were large enough to take these locomotives and the northbound journeys would be run tender first,
hence the tender cabs and the provision of the Whitaker token-
exchanging apparatus on each side of the tenders.

The livery of unlined black and vermilion buffer beams
broke new ground for the Somerset & Dorset and anticipated
the line's standard goods livery of later years. This colouring
suited the class well and gave the appearance of robustness and
power; useful attributes for heavy mineral locomotives. Weak
bridges at the entrance of Bath motive power depot forbade
their using the facilities and initially all had to be shedded at
Radstock until the necessary strengthening had been undertaken. At Radstock, too, there were problems for they fouled
the shed roof so their height was reduced by removing the upper
lip of the chimneys, flattening the dome covers and discarding
the cab roof ventilators. A year or so later the superheater
dampers were found unnecessary and removed while gravity
feed replaced the steam sanding. With a total adhesive weight
of but 56 tons and a factor of adhesion of only 3·5 many
observers thought they would be prone to slipping. But on the
contrary they proved particularly sure-footed on the banks and
when years later a shortage of locomotives necessitated their
use on expresses, they were allowed ten corridor coaches over
the Bath Extension which was two more than the Bulleid
Pacifics.

Their entry into traffic during 1914 must have been most
welcome to the hard-pressed footplate crews for the mineral
resources of the Mendips were being developed as never before.
Coal mined around Radstock had been found excellent for the
manufacture of gas and was in great demand throughout the
West Country while the limestone of Shepton Mallet and Binegar was equally favoured for road construction because of its
readiness to absorb tar.

It was generally expected that the Midland Railway would
build similar 2-8-0s for its own use and with this in mind No
85 was borrowed in March 1918 for trials between Toton and
Brent. It was found capable of performing the work though the

longer distances and high speeds brought to light the axlebox deficiencies. As a result the design was taken as the basis of a class having a maximum axle loading of 17½ tons and the drawings submitted for consideration by the civil engineer. He rejected them because of the excess weight and the scheme was shelved. As far as the Somerset & Dorset was concerned the hot-box problem was solved by fitting No 85 in September 1919 with mechanical lubrication to the coupled boxes. The other five were similarly modified over the next few years, the last being No 82 at Highbridge in April 1924.

The tender cabs proved a mixed blessing, being draughty out in the open and liable to fill with fumes in the tunnels. After consultation with the men it was agreed that they should be removed from one engine for trials. No 82 was in shops at the time so was modified before its return to traffic in December 1918. No 85 was similarly dealt with at Derby in 1919 and all had been altered by the end of 1920.

After World War I the Somerset & Dorset, like most other English railways, was faced with an ever growing onslaught of motor transport. Milk traffic in rural areas was particularly vulnerable, while increasing quantities of road stone were beginning to be transported by road and a number of smaller Somerset collieries were closing down. The country bus was another competitor with an auspicious future and private motoring was developing steadily as more and more rural inhabitants turned to the internal-combustion engine to solve their travelling problems. As a result by January 1922 the line was losing £71,000 yearly and a committee headed by T. Redhead of the Midland Railway was formed to investigate the situation and to suggest means of reducing operating costs. The report dated 17 May 1922 found all the running sheds over-staffed, in some cases by 40 per cent; there was little or no attempt to employ the motive power economically and at least seven engines were in steam daily to provide work for surplus crews rather than to perform a useful function. Highbridge Works also came in for severe criticism because of the acceptance of minor repairs normally performed by running shed staff, the excessive use of new materials and the employment of no less than twenty-one clerks in the office of the locomotive superintendent.

Similar over-staffing was found at the stations, in the signalling department and in the permanent way gangs. It was considered that lasting economies totalling £28,000 per annum could be made without impairing the efficiency of the line and that another £16,000 could be saved if all locomotive repairs were undertaken at Derby and Highbridge Works closed. The report was accepted in its entirety and all the measures suggested put in operation at once, except for the closure of Highbridge which was deferred pending a final decision after the formation of the LMS. Under these circumstances it was obvious that few new locomotives could be provided over the next few years unless their presence was essential for the line's economy.

Five standard Midland Class 4 six-coupled goods had been ordered from Sir W. G. Armstrong, Whitworth & Co Ltd of Scotswood, Newcastle-on-Tyne, at a cost of £10,960 each on 28 July 1920 and when delivered in April 1922 they became Nos 57 to 61. The astronomical rise in building costs in the post-war years is readily apparent when it is recalled that the larger 2-8-0s of 1914 entered traffic priced at £3,500 each. Fortunately, the entire £54,800 did not have to be found because the difference between the charges of 1914 and 1920 was recoverable from the government. By lucky chance these excellent 0-6-0s proved most versatile and could be rostered with equal ease for both the goods and passenger services, which in the summer months virtually gave the line five extra express engines. Indeed, for several decades the standard Somerset & Dorset motive power for the heaviest express duties was a superheated 4-4-0 piloted by one of the Class 4 0-6-0s.

These five engines were identical with a batch of fifty built by the same manufacturer for the Midland. The loading class was shown Derby style as 4, this being quickly altered at Highbridge to 5P4G. Since 1921 black had been the livery of goods engines, these being the first 0-6-0s to enter traffic new so painted. The dimensions were as follows:

Cylinders	20in × 26in
Coupled wheels	5ft 3in
Wheelbase	8ft 0in + 8ft 6in = 16ft 6in
Boiler diameter	4ft 8in
Boiler length	10ft 5$\frac{13}{16}$in
Firebox length	7ft 0in
Boiler pitch	8ft 6in

Heating surfaces:	*sq ft*
Tubes (148 × 1$\frac{3}{4}$in + 21 × 5$\frac{1}{8}$in)	1,045
Firebox	125
Total evaporative	1,170
Superheater	313
Total	1,483

Working pressure	175lb
Grate area	21·1sq ft

Weight in working order:	*tons*	*cwt*
Leading coupled wheels	17	3
Centre coupled wheels	18	0
Trailing coupled wheels	13	12
Engine total	48	15
Tender (3,500gal)	39	18
Engine and tender	88	13

With some justification these 0-6-0s with their G7S superheated boiler and piston valves can be considered an enlarged and much improved variation of the 1875 Johnson design. Their construction was simple and robust, and comparable in size and power with other six-coupled goods currently being built in the country. Nevertheless, it must be borne in mind that many companies had introduced eight-coupled engines for their heaviest goods services. Indeed, Derby had built 2-8-0s for the Somerset & Dorset some years earlier. In traffic they proved

THE LARGE 4-4-0s

Page 153 (*Top*) 4-4-0 No 71 as built in 1903. (*Bottom*) Superheated 4-4-0 No 71 supplied in 1914 as a replacement for the earlier engine

THE JOHNSON 4ft 6in 0-6-0s (THE SCOTTIES)
Page 154   (*Top*) 0-6-0 No 27 built in 1881 by the Vulcan Foundry. (*Bottom*) 0-6-0
No 59 of the 1890 series as reboilered in 1907

THE JOHNSON 5ft 3in 0-6-0s (THE BULLDOGS)
Page 155   (*Top*) 0-6-0 No 66 as built in 1896. (*Bottom*) In its final S & DJR form
No 63 at Highbridge in 1928. This locomotive became LMS No 3198 in 1930 and was
withdrawn in 1947

THE FOX, WALKER SADDLE TANKS

Page 156 (*Top*) 0-6-0ST No 9 of the 1876 series. (*Bottom*) 0-6-0ST No 1 with extended saddle tank as fitted in 1908 on re-conversion to saddle tank form. See p 189 (*top*)

free steaming, reasonably light on fuel and utterly reliable as well as being found even more generally useful than the Bulldogs for they performed equally well as main line goods or express passenger engines.

Surprisingly this was in complete contrast to their reception on the Midland, or later on the LMS, where crews complained of poor steaming and lack of sparkle in their performance. Most crews preferred the Class 3 goods. Possibly the unusual working conditions of the Somerset & Dorset brought out the best in the Armstrongs. Unlike most 0-6-0s pressed into fast passenger service they rode quite well with little shouldering or movement imparted to the leading coaches while there was certainly no lack of speed. Prior to the LMS takeover several other Class 4s were loaned to the Somerset & Dorset, including Nos 3863 and 4275 to 4278.

Passenger, general merchandise and livestock traffic may have been lost to road transport, but the volume of coal and stone passing over the line was greater than in pre-war years. This in turn necessitated working the corresponding trains of empties, providing extra bankers and ensuring the various sidings were supplied with sufficient shunters. By skilfully re-arranging the banking rosters it was found possible to make use of these engines for many of the additional shunting duties in between successive appearances on the main line, but no readjustment of schedules could make more 2-8-0s available. For with one in shops for repair and another on shed for routine maintenance, the maximum number to hand on any day could only be four which regularly made it necessary to employ a pair of 0-6-0s or reduce the loadings by 35 per cent. Therefore, on 30 July 1924 it was decided to take advantage of the recent government compensation payment received under Section II of the Railway Act 1921 to order five more 2-8-0s costing £6,570 each from Robert Stephenson & Co Ltd. It was intended that they would replace five of the small and worn-out Scottie 0-6-0s. They were assembled at this manufacturer's Darlington works and as Nos 86 to 90 were delivered between July and August 1925. No 86 was specially finished off and

painted by the makers for exhibition at the centenary celebra-
tions of the Stockton & Darlington Railway.

These engines differed from the original series by having
boilers 7in larger in diameter, the changed dimensions being as
follows:

Boiler diameter	5ft 3in
Boiler length	11ft 11in
Firebox length	9ft 0in
Boiler pitch	8ft 10in
Heating surfaces:	*sq ft*
Tubes (145 × 1⅞in +	
27 × 5⅛in)	1,323
Firebox	148
	———
Total evaporative	1,471
	———
Superheater	374sq ft
Working pressure	190lb
Grate area	28·4sq ft
Weight in working order:	*tons cwt*

	tons	cwt
Pony truck	9	0
Leading coupled	14	2
Intermediate coupled	15	2
Driving	16	0
Rear coupled	14	7
	———	———
Total engine	68	11
Tender (3,500gal)	42	14
	———	———
Total engine and tender	111	5

The boiler was a non-standard type designated G9BS and
was designed to use the same flanged plates as the boiler fitted to
the 0-10-0 Lickey banking engine; these plates together with
those for the smokebox and the ashpan were produced at
Derby. Ross pop safety valves were fitted while, because of the
larger diameter smokebox, the cast saddle was smaller. Similarly the chimney and dome were shorter on account of the
larger diameter smokebox and boiler. All the chimneys were
cast at Derby, and supplied to the builders.

The tenders were a Fowler standard LMS high-sided design carrying 5½ tons of fuel and 3,500gal of water. They had certain items of water pick-up apparatus fitted and could have been fitted for use with water troughs if required.

Less obvious changes were the provision of left-hand drive, with hand-operated screw reversing and the fitting of Lambert sanding apparatus. This latter was of French design and supplied a mixture of sand and water to the rail. Advantages claimed for the system were that the sand need not be dried before use, did not blow off the rails in cross winds and the apparatus could be set to give a series of drops of sand/water mixture while running on greasy rails.

Following delivery of these engines the original series were modified to bring them into line. The steam-operated reversing gear was replaced by hand-operated screws, although right-hand drive was retained. The first engine to be so treated was No 84 in March 1926. At the same time the cab roofs were extended back over the tenders.

The LMS in 1924 wished to supersede double heading of the Nottinghamshire–London coal trains of the Midland Division. This was the heaviest regular mineral traffic on the LMS, but, unfortunately, was subject to severe width and weight limitations, and it was found impossible, with the technique available at the time, to adapt a proposed four-cylinder Lancashire & Yorkshire 2-10-0 design. A 2-8-2 was then considered and when this too failed to pass the civil engineer, the problem was left unsolved until 1926 when the Lickey incline 0-10-0 No 2290 was tried over part of the route. It proved quite incapable of main line work, so three Beyer Peacock 2-6-0:0-6-2 Garratts were ordered for delivery in 1927. Although the boiler and frame design was Beyer's, all the detail work was to Derby requirements based on the Somerset & Dorset design which ensured they worked throughout their existence under the burden of short travel valve gear, undersized Class 4 coupled boxes and no guiding wheels at the inner ends of the units. Thirty more of these engines were delivered in 1930, double exhaust valves giving a slight improvement in efficiency. They successfully handled the Toton–Brent coal trains, doing the work of two 0-6-0s, but with no great advantage as regards efficiency, apart from the saving of two men's wages.

For obvious reasons these Garratts were unsuitable for freight service elsewhere on the LMS, so in 1927 it was decided that the company's heavy goods engine should be eight coupled with a moderate axle load and a tractive power similar to that of the ex-LNWR G2 class. This was the last development of 0-8-0s on the North Western which down the years had hauled mineral trains, slowly, reliably, and without fuss. To the connoisseur of locomotive design they appeared crude and uninspiring, thus Derby confidently anticipated that the Somerset & Dorset 2-8-0 would excel in a series of trials held over the Midland route of Toton–Syston–Melton Mowbray–Kettering–Bedford–Brent. However, incredibly to many observers, 2-8-0 No 88 came out worst. It was at once taken out of service and dispatched to Derby where the valves were cleaned and adjusted before more trials were held. Meanwhile G2s Nos 9409 and 9428 were performing quite satisfactorily. These trials were conducted on normal trains, not constant speed controlled services, but like against like train on alternate days. Therefore, to some extent the results could be influenced by weather, coasting down hills and good fortune with signals. Notwithstanding the results obtained, taking all outside influences into account, probably offered a reasonably accurate assessment of the two classes. Although to Derby's everlasting chagrin the G2s still gave the best results. Details of these trials are opposite.

After due consideration it was decided to construct the 9500 Class 0-8-0s using the G2 class as the basis of their design. The boiler remained, although increased to 200lb pressure, but the chassis was replanned with new cylinders and inside long travel Walschaerts gear. The effect of the improved steam distribution was very marked, but the handicap of high piston loads on Class 4 axleboxes prevented them giving the required high mileages between successive repairs with the result that they were relegated to secondary work as soon as the Stanier 2-8-0s entered service.

Engine class	2-6-0 : 2-6-0 Garratt	2-8-0 S & D	0-8-0 LNWR	0-8-0 Standard LMS
From individual costs averaged over 10 years				
Coal per mile (lb)	116·6	—	74·6	69·9
Repair cost index (a)	202	—(b)	156	124
Average load (tons)	1,452	927	940	900
„ running speed (mph)	16·0	17·5	17·6	17·3
Coal consumption (lb per mile)	112·6	80·6	79·0	53·9
lb per ton mile	0·07	0·078	0·076	0·055
lb per DBHP/hr	3·61	4·37	4·02	2·80
lb per sq ft grate/hr	40·6	49·5	49·0	39·4
Water consumption				
gal per mile	84·6	60·8	50·0	46·1
lb per DBHP/hr	27·1	32·9	25·4	24·0
Evaporation (lb water per lb of coal)	7·51	7·54	6·32	8·57

(a) The Midland Class 2 4-4-0 was taken at 100.

(b) No comparable figures were available, although they were estimated as 77·2 and 62 respectively.

On the Somerset & Dorset the shortcomings of the undersized axleboxes and outmoded valve gear was never readily apparent, and the class averaged 56,000 miles between general repairs. However, the coal consumption remained high at 87·4lb per mile. Of more immediate concern was the lack of spare boilers, so to alleviate the position two second-hand Compound boilers were modified at Derby and fitted to Nos 84 and 85 in November and December 1929. The two displaced boilers were repaired, but instead of being retained as intended to form a float of spares, they were used in February and March 1930 to reboiler Nos 89 and 90 of the second and larger-boilered series. Because of the changed diameter it was necessary to insert a packing piece on the smokebox saddle to carry the smaller smokebox. As there were now five G9BS boilers for Nos 86 to 88 and no spare G9AS pattern for Nos 80 to 85, 89 and 90, Derby modified two more Compound boilers to ease the repair situation. It was 1947 before a free exchange of boilers was established with the LMS and Midland Compounds.

On 20 November 1929 No 89 ran away into Bath when heading the 3.25pm goods from Evercreech. The crew were overcome by the fumes in Combe Down tunnel and the train with no one at the controls gathered speed as it hurtled down the bank pushed by thirty-seven wagons until derailment occurred at the entrance to Bath goods yard. Destruction was great, although only Driver Jennings, the yard inspector and an LMS clerk were killed. At the inquiry the fireman explained how the engine was steaming so badly that he had been forced to sit down and wrap his head in his coat, after which he recalled nothing until the derailment. To avoid a recurrence of the disaster various trial runs were made with the 2-8-0s and Class 4 goods through Combe Down tunnel to evaluate the atmosphere, which in certain weather conditions was found particularly bad, although not sufficient to offer a hazard unless an engine was steaming unusually poorly. Henceforth care was to be taken to avoid employing engines in such condition and to supply all heavy freight engines with good quality fuel.

Supervision of Somerset & Dorset motive power remained with Derby after the 1923 grouping, which left Fowler in charge until 20 July 1927 when he resigned on finding the work of chief mechanical engineer of the LMS left no time for the Joint line. His successor, S. J. Symes, was the works superintendent of the Midland Division (LMS). Because of the working losses no new passenger engines had been received for six years and the position regarding motive power was precarious. A report on the locomotive stock was called for in December 1927 and when presented the following May it recommended that twelve goods and two passenger engines aged from 37 to 54 years should be broken up as they were not worth the expense of new boilers, frames and cylinders. They should be replaced by seven standard LMS six-coupled tanks at £3,000 each and three superheated 4-4-0s at £5,000 each. Their introduction and the extension of the washout periods should enable £8,750 per annum being saved by the reduction of five in the locomotive stock to 81. An additional saving of £1,086 was envisaged by the combining of LMS and Joint motive power establishments at Bath while no less than £29,000 yearly would be saved by closing the works at Highbridge and transferring all light repairs to Bristol and general overhauls to Derby. After consideration these findings, apart from the Highbridge closure, were accepted and the ten new locomotives ordered while on 19 July 1928 two Sentinel shunters for service at Radstock in place of the Dazzlers were added to the list.

The standard Fowler Jinty 0-6-0 tanks were built by W. G. Bagnall Ltd of Stafford who at the time were supplying similar engines to the LMS. They were delivered as Nos 19 to 25 between December 1928 and February 1929. Probably on account of the several roles they were expected to fill, as bankers, shunters, short distance goods and local passenger engines, all were painted unlined blue instead of the black usually applied to goods stock. Their dimensions were as follows:

Cylinders	18in × 26in
Coupled wheels	4ft 7in
Wheelbase	8ft 0in + 8ft 6in = 16ft 6in
Boiler diameter	4ft 1in
Boiler length	10ft 6in
Firebox length	5ft 6in
Boiler pitch	7ft 4½in
Heating surfaces:	*sq ft*
Tubes (194 × 1¾in)	967½
Firebox	97
Total	1,064½
Working pressure	160lb
Grate area	16sq ft

Weight in working order:	*tons*	*cwt*
Leading coupled wheels	14	3
Centre coupled wheels	17	14
Trailing coupled wheels	17	13
Total	49	10

Water capacity	1,200gal
Bunker capacity	2¼ tons

Their design was directly derived from Johnson's 'S' class of 1899 which in turn owed much to this engineer's six-coupled tanks of 1874, so the Jinties could justifiably claim to be the final version of these Midland engines. The G5½ boiler was of Derby design and probably the best of its size on the LMS. Reversing was by screw while steam carriage heating and vacuum brake equipment was fitted to cover their local passenger duties.

On 1 January 1930 all Somerset & Dorset locomotives were taken into LMS stock, the Class 4 0-6-0s, Jinties and 2-8-0s being renumbered as follows:

S & DJR Nos	Type	1st LMS Nos	2nd LMS Nos	British Railways Nos
57 to 61	0-6-0	4557 to 4561	—	44557 to 44561
19 to 25	0-6-0T	7150 to 7156	7310 to 7316 (1934)	47310 to 47316
80 to 90	2-8-0	9670 to 9680	13800 to 13810 (1932)	53800 to 53810

Each class will now be taken in turn and their history given under LMS and British Railways ownership. It was coincidental not design that the Armstrong 0-6-0s retained their last two figures unchanged when they became Nos 4557 to 4561. Under Somerset & Dorset control they kept their own boilers, but now there was a regular exchange with other engines carrying the same pattern and this in course of time led to the Ramsbottom safety valves giving way to Ross pops, the appearance of lower dome covers and shorter Stanier chimneys without capuchons. Additional weather angles were also welded to the cab roof just above the side look-out to prevent rain running off the roof and into the driver's face when looking out of the cab. During the mid-1930s the piston tail rods were removed, the covers taken off the buffer beams and the holes blanked over.

Throughout the 1930s the LMS left all five at Bath and even during World War II, when many Somerset & Dorset section engines had to be transferred away and replaced by various Southern Railway classes, their retention was still considered essential. All entered British Railways stock and became Nos 44557 to 44561 when next in shops.

At Derby in February 1956 No 44561 was coupled to tender No 2762 ex-Compound No 41123 which had commenced service behind a Midland Belpaire (Class 3) 4-4-0. It was of the standard Johnson bogie variety, but in March 1913 was rebuilt as a 3,500gal, six-wheeled tender with a 13ft 9in wheelbase and transferred to Class 3 No 732 where it remained until this engine was withdrawn in 1929. Subsequently it passed to Compound No 1197 and in May 1937 was rebuilt with a Fowler tank of the pattern used on LMS standard 13ft 0in wheelbase tenders, which left a platform at the rear between the back of the tank and the buffer beam. By October 1950 it was partnered by Compound No 41123 and as stated above later gravitated to No 44561. Nos 44558 to 44560 also received spare tenders with histories of varying degrees of complication.

Nationalisation did little to change their mode of life before April 1962 when No 44561 was withdrawn with a mileage of 1,008,768. In the following August, No 44557 was transferred to Carlisle, although this was only a paper transaction for withdrawal occurred in September 1962. Nos 44558 and 44559 were similarly discarded in 1963–4, but not before the former and 2-8-0 No 53808 had worked the last public service train headed by ex-S & DJR engines on 6 June 1964. Farewell specials ran over the line for some years for the Somerset & Dorset took an unconscionable time a-dying. One on 28 March 1965 was in charge of No 44560 which three months later was transferred to Gloucester before withdrawal in August 1965.

The blue livery of Jinties Nos 7150 to 7156 soon gave way to LMS black with a subsequent lowering of cleaning standards. For much of 1930 No 7156 ran with both its old Somerset & Dorset and new LMS numbers on the smokebox door. They proved most useful and in course of time became worthy substitutes for the Fox, Walker saddle tanks. Nos 7155 and 7156 were quickly transferred to Plaistow and, although both had returned by mid-1931, they must have left a good impression in East London for Nos 7310 to 7315 were soon to be seen working from Devons Road on the passenger services out of Broad Street, including those over the LNER (ex-Great Northern) suburban lines. Devons Road was a great stronghold of LMS screw reverse Jinties, so presumably the opportunity was taken to increase their numbers and replace them on the Somerset & Dorset by surplus lever reverse Jinties which would be restricted to shunting or banking activities. Destination board brackets were fitted for use on the Broad Street services while several, including Nos 7310 and 7315, received Strowger-Hudd ATC equipment so use could be made of them over the Tilbury section. Around the same period No 7316 was transferred to Bristol.

Later these seven engines saw service on the Lickey incline, from Burton, Gloucester and elsewhere while No 47316 returned to the Somerset & Dorset and was the only one withdrawn from there in November 1962. All had been scrapped by the end of 1966 except for No 47313 which not only outlasted them but almost all other ex-Midland-designed engines as well. For stationed at Westhouses, Nottinghamshire, it was one of four six-coupled tanks employed shunting some ten miles away at Williamthorpe Colliery until June 1967, several months after the remainder of the class had gone the way of all old engines. Latterly Stanier chimneys had replaced the Deeley variety.

During the 1930s various modifications befell the 2-8-os including the fitting of Ross pop safety valves to the original series and trials with Kylala blast pipes and large-diameter chimneys on Nos 13802/4 from 1932 to 1934. Snifting valves were fitted in place of the Fowler–Anderson by-pass valves, new tyres were fitted, increasing the wheel diameter to 4ft 8½in and the brakes were removed from the pony trucks. Just before the war the whole class were fitted with steam sanding gear, double-handled regulators and LMS standard sliding firebox doors while the Deeley pattern chimneys were similarly replaced by those of Stanier design.

With the formation of British Railways in 1948 they had 40,000 added to their numbers and became 53800 to 53810. Reboilering of the second series with the G9AS pattern was completed during the 1950s; the dates being No 53806 in August 1955, No 53807 in June 1954 and No 53808 in December 1953. When No 53807 was reboilered it was found that the smokebox saddle was badly corroded and a new one was cast to the 1914 design.

Under the Somerset & Dorset power classification system the 2-8-0s were 5P5G but it is doubtful if the passenger symbol meant very much at first. The Derby title of 'Mineral Engine' shows the work for which they were intended but they did pass on to passenger work, probably by way of working pigeon specials and were allowed to take ten coaches unaided over the Mendips. In the early 1950s the flood of through trains over the line taxed the locomotive department to the full and it was agreed that the 2-8-0s could be used to ease the need for pilots. Such working endeared them to the photographers and the enthusiasts, but it must have shortened their lives.

By 1959 only No 53804 of the original series had retained an original Deeley tender. Standard LMS Fowler tenders of 13ft 0in wheelbase had been fitted to Nos 53801/2/3/5 while No 53800 had acquired a Deeley 13ft 9in wheelbase tender with a Fowler short tank. The original tender of No 53805 was attached to the preserved Midland Compound No 1000 at the time of its restoration and is now exhibited in Clapham Museum. In 1959 No 53804 still carried its original MR works plates of 1914 and was probably the last locomotive to run so adorned.

Withdrawal started in 1959 with No 53800 but no more were taken out of service until No 53802 was withdrawn in 1960. The remainder of the first series were withdrawn during 1961-2 and all were sent to either Crewe or Doncaster for cutting-up. The second series were withdrawn during 1963-4 and were sold to contractors to be cut-up. Fortunately, not all were broken up immediately and a fund was opened to preserve No 53808 which was removed from the scrap yard and stored by Woodham Brothers next to the Dart Valley's No 7827 *Lydney Manor* in the former Barry goods depot. In October 1970 it was moved to Bristol for display at the Bath Road Open Day and thence to Radstock for restoration by The Somerset & Dorset Railway Circle.

CHAPTER TEN

THE TRAIN SERVICES

The pattern of train services developed as the line grew, reaching a peak about 1914. Although most services were reinstated after the war a gradual decline set in relieved only by a short revival after World War II. The eventual rundown and closure became inevitable when British Railways was set financial viability as its goal.

Original services on the Somerset Central Railway were run by the Bristol & Exeter and were designed to connect with the latter company's trains at Highbridge. The simple service involved no crossings and could be worked by one engine and set of stock. There were six trains a day in each direction with two on Sundays. Most of these were allowed thirty-five minutes for the 12 mile journey, but two were booked at twenty-five minutes.

The Burnham Extension was operated as a separate branch with trains running to Highbridge to connect with the Bristol & Exeter rather than the trains to Glastonbury. Originally there were nine departures a day from Burnham, two or three on Sundays, but only six arrivals. By 1861 this had increased to eleven trains a day in each direction with one or two on Sundays.

With the opening of the Wells Extension the service pattern was changed so that the trains ran through from Highbridge to Wells. By 1861 there were seven trains a day each way, two on Sundays, and of these seven only two stopped at Ashcott and Bason Bridge while others did not stop at Edington Road. Most trains took from thirty-eight to sixty minutes for the $17\frac{1}{2}$

mile journey, but the 6am from Wells stopped only at Glastonbury and was allowed thirty-five minutes.

Dorset Central services were originally worked by the London
& South Western Railway and again were designed to require
a minimum of stock. Services started and finished at Blandford
so the locomotives presumably returned to Wimborne for overnight stabling. The 10 mile journey from Wimborne to the
temporary station at Blandford St Mary took from thirty to
thirty-five minutes inclusive of two stops. There were five trains
a day in each direction with two on Sundays.

By 1863 the line to Templecombe was complete with mixed
gauge on the Somerset Central. Trains were now run to Burnham and Highbridge using newly acquired narrow-gauge stock.
There were five trains a day each way, two on Sundays, the
first train out and the last in at Templecombe using the Lower
Station only. All other trains proceeded to the Upper Station
after calling at the Lower. The best train took 1hr 42min for
the 35 miles from Burnham, this including a wait at Highbridge
and reversals to reach Templecombe Upper. Most trains took
about 2hr for this journey inclusive of ten stops.

There were five trains a day each way from Wells to Highbridge and the Bristol & Exeter ran two broad-gauge trains a
day. The passenger train ran from Bristol to Wells via Highbridge while the goods train left Bristol at 10.30pm, worked to
Wells via Highbridge, returned to Glastonbury and then
worked to Evercreech over the Bruton Extension. This train
was later re-scheduled to leave Bristol at 3.30am but both
ceased to run after 1868.

The long-awaited Channel-to-Channel route was finally
obtained with the opening of the Templecombe–Blandford
section in 1863. There were four through trains a day each way
from Burnham to Hamworthy (for Poole) with two on Sundays. The best times were Hamworthy to Highbridge in 3hr
15min and Burnham to Hamworthy in 3hr 50min. Most trains
were scheduled to take 4hr for the 70 mile journey which included a reversal at Wimborne. At that time through trains
called only at Templecombe Lower and the LSWR ran a shuttle

service to the Upper Station. From 1867, however, all trains called at the Upper involving another set of reversals. There were also local trains between Burnham and Highbridge, Burnham and Wells and from either Templecombe or Blandford to Wimborne.

In the summer of 1864 another through train was added from Burnham to Hamworthy while one of the Sunday trains was accelerated to reach Hamworthy in 3hr 20min from Burnham. This was followed by a recession and by 1874 the services had been run down, to such an extent that there were no Sunday trains and only three through trains from Burnham to the new station at Poole.

Following this recession the opening of the Bath Extension changed the emphasis of working and the main trains ran from Bath to Bournemouth. There were four through trains a day with two carrying through coaches from Birmingham. The services were timed from three to four hours for the 74 mile journey except for one train in each direction which was scheduled to complete it in under three hours. These two trains were allowed seventy-five minutes for the single-line section between Bath and Templecombe. There were six daily goods trains over the line and from 1877 a stone train was run from either Binegar or Winsor Hill.

The old main line from Burnham was relegated to a branch with trains running to Templecombe. There were five trains a day with one up train from Bournemouth splitting at Templecombe to form the train to Burnham. There were five daily goods trains over the old main line, three running to Templecombe and two to Wimborne.

From 1876 through coaches to Bournemouth were run from Bradford, Leeds and Sheffield on the Midland Railway and from York and Newcastle via the Midland. By 1884 the services had been improved to six through trains daily from Bath to Bournemouth with the 2.30pm down train reaching Bournemouth in 2hr 34min, including eight stops and a reversal at Wimborne. Ten years later the building of the Corfe Mullen cut-off and the doubling of some sections of track enabled this time to be reduced to 2hr 20min with eight stops, and the 9.40am up train now took 2hr 10min to reach Bath with seven stops. There were now seven through trains a day in each direction.

By 1884 goods traffic had increased to twelve trains a day from Bath to Templecombe and three from Templecombe to Wimborne, one of these latter being a mixed train. In May 1888 the 2.30am goods from Bath to Templecombe was changed to become the 2.50am express night goods and mail train to Bournemouth, the title express being a little misleading as the train took a little under five hours for the journey. In this mixed form this continued to be the main night train over the Somerset & Dorset up to 1964.

The Bridgwater Railway was opened in 1890 and two fast trains were run to Templecombe each day to connect with the Waterloo expresses. The trains were run in competition with the Great Western service to Paddington via Bristol and one of the trains ran the 35 miles from Templecombe to Bridgwater in sixty-six minutes, stopping only at Glastonbury and Edington Junction.

In 1894 there were seventeen goods trains a day over the main line comprising nine through goods to Templecombe, three to Evercreech Junction, four local goods and the night mail. The number of goods trains run at night had increased and five up trains left Templecombe between 12.10am and 3.45am.

Doubling of further sections of the main line and the introduction of the Whitaker token-exchange apparatus enabled a further increase in speed and by 1904 the Bournemouth Express took only 2hr 2min from Bath with three stops. In the reverse direction the 'North Express' took 2hr 3min with six stops and in the summer timetable this was improved to give two expresses each way in 1hr 50min. A relief train running on Mondays and Thursdays only set an all time record for the journey of 1hr 47min and this was scheduled to run non-stop from Poole to Bath in ninety-six minutes. The goods services had also increased and by this time there were twenty-one down trains each day from Bath as well as five mineral trains from Radstock, Binegar or Winsor Hill.

The timetable for 1914 offered the best all year round service on the main line with seven through trains in the down direction and ten in the up direction. There were five extra stopping trains on each half of the line with some running via Wimborne in the down direction but only one up train calling there. The Manchester Express was introduced in 1910 running from Bath to Bournemouth in 1hr 50min and in the up direction to Bath in 2hr 10min. In 1927 this train was officially named the Pines Express.

The branch services comprised five down and seven up trains each day, some running to Templecombe while there was a service of eighteen trains each way between Burnham and Highbridge. The Bridgwater line had become a branch with six trains a day each way while the Wells branch had ten trains a day each way with one through working to Highbridge.

Services were drastically curtailed during World War I and took time to return afterwards. The Wimborne line was down to one train a day and this was withdrawn in July 1920. By 1924 the main line services were almost back to pre-war standards with two daily expresses for the North and four additional ones at summer weekends. A through train from Burnham to Bournemouth was run for a while taking 3hr 13min down and 2hr 47min up. On the freight side traffic continued to increase and many more trains were run at night.

The basic pattern of services was now set, but during the 1930s there was a large increase in excursion traffic especially at summer weekends. A number of trains were run from Bristol to Bournemouth and a daily express from Temple Meads taking 2hr 46min down and 2hr 57min up. At summer weekends there were large numbers of through trains from the North but all this ceased with the onset of hostilities in 1939. Services were reduced to four trains a day each way on the main line, stopping at all stations, and three or four trains daily on the branch.

After the war there was a slow return to normality, but in 1951–2 Burnham, Wells and Bridgwater lost their services.

F

This was the beginning of the major reduction, but for a time during the 1950s through traffic on summer Saturdays was as heavy as the line could cope with. Finally the run-down came with the withdrawal of through services in 1962 and final closure in 1966.

1930 TO THE END

With their absorption into LMS stock on 1 January 1930, the
Somerset & Dorset locomotives lost their identity while the distinctive blue livery of the passenger classes rapidly gave way to
black. A detailed list of the eighty locomotives concerned and
their LMS numbers will be found in the Appendix.

At the same time the running sheds came under the administration of the Midland Division and were allotted the following
code numbers: M5 Templecombe; M6 Highbridge with the
sub-sheds of Wells and Bridgwater; M8 Bristol of which the
combined Midland and Joint sheds at Bath, together with those
at Radstock and Bournemouth, were sub-sheds. The 'M' prefix
did not appear on the smokebox door shed-plates, it being
employed only in correspondence and the official records to
avoid confusion with similarly numbered sheds of the other
LMS Divisions.

Between 1930 and 1938 no major change was made to the
locomotive policy, although the small Scottie 0-6-0s were
soon withdrawn. Therefore, the main line passenger services
remained in charge of the 2P 4-4-0s with the powerful 7F 2-8-0s
working the heavy mineral trains and the versatile 4F 0-6-0s
undertaking many mixed traffic duties. On the branch and
south of Templecombe the 0-4-4 tanks and the smaller 0-6-0s
fulfilled most of the lighter tasks. Economy of working was
essential, so when locomotives were withdrawn they were replaced cheaply by similar-sized LMS classes, as for example
when the Joint 0-4-4 tanks left for scrapping their duties were
taken over by ex-Midland engines of that type. There were odd

exceptions to the rule, as for instance in 1931 when Kirtley double-framed 0-6-0s Nos 2687 and 2817 replaced Scotties Nos 2886 and 2888 while for some months in the following year ex-Midland 2-4-0 No 155 worked from Templecombe.

During 1933 a programme of bridge strengthening was carried out on the main line and on the branch, and although this had no immediate effect it did pave the way for later improvements. At the same time Bath Shed was modernised and the track of the Wimborne line removed. In 1935 the new Stanier Class 5 4-6-0s began working into Bristol and it was agreed that all the weak bridges on the Mangotsfield–Bath line should be rebuilt to allow them into Bath and thence over the Somerset & Dorset. In the same year the turntable at Bath was replaced by one of 60ft diameter to enable the larger locomotives, including the 2-8-0s, to be turned. The LMS revised its Motive Power Depot codes that year with the result that the entire Somerset & Dorset line came under the control of Bristol thus:

Bristol:	22A
Gloucester:	22B
Bath:	22C (sub-shed Radstock)
Templecombe:	22D
Highbridge:	22E (sub-sheds Wells, Bridgwater)

It is interesting to note that the Bristol District locomotive superintendent was A. H. Whitaker, the son of the former Joint line's resident locomotive superintendent, and he had been in charge at Bath for a number of years. Heavy running repairs to locomotives were now undertaken at Bristol with only light repairs and routine maintenance being carried out at the sub-sheds.

Towards the end of 1935 trials were held with ex-London, Tilbury & Southend 4-4-2 tank No 2103. It was stationed at Templecombe and worked a daily roster which included a journey up the branch to Highbridge and Burnham in the morning and a trip to Bath and back in the afternoon. Following these trials it was tried on the Bath–Bristol services. Although it rode well and provided a marginal increase in power over the

0-4-4 tanks it was very heavy on coal and was said to prime badly. After leaving the area its duties were taken over by 0-4-4 tank No 1387.

By the beginning of 1938 the bridges on the Mangotsfield–Bath line had been rebuilt and the Stanier Class 5 4-6-0s could now work right through to Bournemouth. Trials over the Somerset & Dorset were run in March of that year with No 5228 and for the summer services six of the class were allocated to Bath. They entered regular traffic on 2 May with No 5432 being the first on the 10.20am Bath–Bournemouth semi-fast and No 5440 on the Pines Express. The latter was to become a regular Somerset & Dorset locomotive and was one of the last two Stanier Class 5s to leave the line in 1958.

The introduction of the Class 5 4-6-0s was designed to enable the normal formation of the Pines Express to be taken without the need of a pilot. The Class 2P 4-4-0s were allowed to take 210 tons unaided over the Mendips and the Class 4F 0-6-0s 240 tons, while the limit for the Class 5s was set at 270 tons. As long as six-coach formations provided sufficient accommodation then the 2P 4-4-0s could cope satisfactorily, but when eight coaches became necessary at busy periods then resort had to be made to the 4F 0-6-0s while should this formation include one of the heavy twelve-wheeled dining cars then a pilot engine had to be found. The combination of a 2P and 4F was truly formidable, but only at the expense of two extra wages and a coal consumption of some 90 to 95lb of coal per mile. In traffic the Class 5s were found capable in all weathers of handling the heaviest of these eight-coach formations and at once became firm favourites with the men. One rarely heard a bad word spoken of them in spite of the fact that some very run-down specimens were encountered at times.

The LMS under Stanier decided in October 1935 to replace the Somerset & Dorset locomotive stock with more modern designs and the Class 5s were the first part of this programme. At about the same time three of the Stanier Class 3 2-6-2 tanks were sent to the line. They were Nos 179 to 181 and were shedded at Bath and Templecombe for use on local passenger

trains and banking duties out of Bath. In 1941 three of the
Stanier 8F 2-8-0s were allocated to Bath but at that time they
were urgently needed elsewhere and were soon taken away. In
any case their brake power was much inferior to the 7F 2-8-0s
and this restricted their use on the heavy mineral services.

The onset of hostilities in 1939 cut short this modernisation
programme and most of the Class 5s were taken away. As a
temporary substitute Compound 4-4-0 No 1046 was sent, but
it seems to have been used only on semi-fasts and locals. The
LMS urgently required more motive power for the line so they
approached the Southern Railway who at the time possessed a
sizeable surplus of engines because of the reduced wartime
passenger services. After some negotiation Drummond S11
Class 4-4-0s Nos 395 to 404 and T9 Class No 304 were transferred for main line duties while Adams T1 Class 0-4-4 tanks
Nos 1 to 6 took over much of the local work. The 4-4-0s were
very robustly constructed and local fitters commented on the
weight of the motion parts as compared with the LMS 2PS.
Several Stirling 4-4-0s also saw brief service on the line during
passage on loan from the Southern while later a number of the
S11s were transferred to Gloucester—such was the LMS locomotive shortage.

During 1942 ex-Lancashire & Yorkshire 0-4-0 saddle tank
No 11202 was again working at Radstock, on this occasion to
replace Sentinel No 7191 which was required at Highbridge to
shunt the wharf and the newly laid government petrol storage
sidings. By 1943 the motive power situation was less critical and
sundry LMS 'Crab' 2-6-0s appeared on the Somerset & Dorset
to take charge of the main trains until replaced in the following
year by Class 5s, including the newly built No 4844 and old
friend No 5440. With the cessation of hostilities in 1945, LMS
locomotives returned in force and those on loan from the
Southern were sent home, although T9 4-4-0s did reappear on
several occasions deputising for failed engines on the Bournemouth–Bath services.

The Transport Act was passed during August 1947 and from
1 January 1948 all railways were grouped together to form

British Railways. From 2 February 1948 the Somerset & Dorset was placed in the Southern Region with the London Midland Region responsible for motive power. This meant little or no change as far as the locomotives were concerned, although later in the year Ivatt 4MT 2-6-0 No 43012 was borrowed from Bristol on Saturdays to help out with the holiday traffic. In subsequent years this engine was allocated to Bath along with Nos 43013, 43017 and 43036. In their original double chimney guise they proved erratic steamers and tended to be employed piloting instead of as main line engines. However, it was a very different story when Class 2 2-6-2 tanks Nos 41240 to 41243 arrived new at Bath towards the end of 1949. They immediately took over all the local turns, including those from Bath to Bristol, while early in the New Year No 41241 was transferred to Templecombe for service on the branch. Being comfortable to ride on, with free steaming boilers and easy maintenance they proved readily acceptable to the men and members of the class were in use right down to closure in 1966.

At the beginning of January 1950 the regional boundaries were redrawn and that section of the Somerset & Dorset north of Cole was added to the Western Region. This was followed in February 1950 by the transfer of the locomotive depots to the Southern Region, the locomotive stock still being loaned by the LMR. This necessitated the depots being renumbered into the '71' Eastleigh series as follows:

Bath:	71G (sub-shed Radstock)
Templecombe:	71H
Highbridge:	71J

During early 1950 an ex-Midland Class 3P 4-4-0 No 40741 appeared for trials, but as the increase in power over the Class 2P 4-4-0s was only marginal it was soon returned to the LMR. A forecast of the Southern Region's intention to use their own motive power over the line came on 1 May 1950 when a U Class 2-6-0 No 31624 piloted Class 5 4-6-0 No 44839 in both directions on the Pines Express. The Western Region, however, placed a 45mph speed restriction on the class over the Somerset

& Dorset so its use was ruled out for most passenger duties. As a
result resort that summer for the first time had to be made to
rostering the 7F 2-8-0s regularly for the Saturday through services. To the surprise of some and the delight of many they
proved worthy of their elevated role. As a possible replacement
for the LMS Class 5s an unrebuilt Bulleid light Pacific, No 34109
Sir Trafford Leigh Mallory, was given a series of trial runs over the
line during March 1951. These started with the seven-coach
semi-fasts to Bristol and concluded with working the ten-coach
Pines Express unaided to and from Bournemouth. This proved
to be almost too much for the engine and although the tests
were officially considered satisfactory the load limit was set at
270 tons unaided over the Mendips. Their nominal increase in
power over the Class 5s was offset by their lack of adhesion, and
since on summer Saturdays they were often in the hands of
crews who were completely unfamiliar with their eccentricities,
the use of pilots was essential. However, Nos 34040/1/2/3 were
allocated to Bath for the summer and on Saturdays more were
frequently borrowed from Bournemouth.

During 1951 the old locomotive shed at Templecombe was
replaced by a new brick building. The former, and the Somerset
& Dorset shed at Bath, were of timber and asbestos construction
and it has often been commented that the most surprising thing
was that their framing was never set alight by sparks or hot
ashes. The Wells branch was closed on 29 October 1951 and
passenger services were withdrawn from the Highbridge–
Burnham line. This signalled the start of withdrawal of the
0-4-4 tanks from the line and the 3F 0-6-0s were increasingly
used on the passenger services over the branch.

The pattern of services set in 1951 was continued through
1952–3. The line was worked as economically as possible during
the winter followed by an allocation of light Pacifics for the
summer with plenty of borrowing of locomotives at Bath and
Bournemouth on Saturdays. The number of trains passing over
the line on these occasions rose to such proportions that it was
necessary to continue using the 2-8-0s and they could be relied
upon to take ten coaches unaided over the Mendips although

they tended to cause delays on the single-line sections in Dorset.

Further test runs were made with Maunsell 2-6-0s during March 1954. The engines involved were Class U No 31621 and Class U1 No 31906, but nothing came of these trials and in May some of the new BR Class 5 4-6-0s Nos 73050 to 73052 were allocated to Bath. Being slightly heavier than the Black 5s, the Western Region placed a 45mph speed restriction for these locomotives over three bridges near Bath. Being similar to the earlier 4-6-0s the crews accepted them readily and soon found that they were very free running, No 73052 being timed at 80mph through Bailey Gate with a twelve-coach down express.

Early in 1955 a second BR class started to make regular appearances on the line. The locomotives involved were shedded at Eastleigh and were the Class 4 2-6-0s. The duty involved working the last up passenger train from Bournemouth to Bath, an overnight stay at Bath, and then a return with the first down passenger to Bournemouth the following morning. At the end of April 1955 Bath suffered a motive power shortage and for a short period 0-4-4 tank No 58072 was used to work local passenger trains, while for the summer two further BR Class 5s were loaned to Bath from Nine Elms. They were Nos 73071/3, but it was still found necessary to borrow heavily on summer Saturdays, so for 1956 several of the BR Class 4 4-6-0s were transferred from Exmouth Junction to Bath. These were Nos 75070/1/2, but it was No 75073 which arrived in place of No 75070 which was under repair. During the winter months these engines took over the local and semi-fast services from the 2P, 4-4-0s, although piloting the Pines Express steadfastly remained a 4-4-0 duty. During 1957 a further series of BR Class 5s were allocated to Bath to replace some of the Stanier engines and for the summer of 1958 two more, Nos 73087 and 73116, were loaned from Nine Elms and Stewarts Lane.

The main event of 1958, as far as Somerset & Dorset motive power was concerned, was the takeover by the Western Region. Control of motive power now came under Bristol (Bath Road) and the motive power depots were renumbered in the '82' series thus:

Bath: 82F (sub-sheds Radstock
                           and Highbridge)
Templecombe: 82G

One of the first changes was to replace the two remaining Stanier Class 5s with BR locomotives and at long last No 45440 was forced to leave the line although it had previously been away for a short period during the war. This was not the end of the Stanier Class 5s for during the summer it was usual to 'borrow' at least one which had reached Bath from the North for a working to Bournemouth and back on Saturdays.

Highbridge shed was officially closed on 11 May 1959 although locomotives continued to be stabled there overnight. At the beginning of the year trials were conducted with Western Region locomotives of various types. Those involved were 0-6-0 No 2251 and 0-6-0 pannier-tanks Nos 3604 and 8451. A 2-8-0 of the Riddles Austerity design was also tried, but was lacking in brake power, and when it finally became necessary to replace the 7F 2-8-0s the Stanier 8F engines took over.

Having seen the problems of working trains over the steeply graded main line the Western Region took a bold step. During March 1960 trials were run with Class 9 2-10-0 No 92204 and for the summer Nos 92203 to 92206 were allocated to Bath. The decision to employ freight engines regularly on passenger duties was justified by the fact that locomotives of this class had proved particularly free running when they had deputised for failed passenger engines, and they would have the power to climb the hills. The load for an unaided Class 9 was initially set at 390 tons, though on several occasions much heavier trains were worked without assistance and the limit was raised to 400 and eventually to 410 tons. The locomotives allocated to the Somerset & Dorset all had double chimneys and this fact undoubtedly helped their steaming, especially when being worked hard with poor quality coal. After so many years the line had

finally acquired engines which could work the main trains unaided even though they had grown to twelve coaches.

During 1960 some Western Region 0-6-0s were sent to replace
the locomotives which were being scrapped. We thus had the
coincidence of No 3218 being sent to Templecombe to replace
No 43218. Although nominally of greater power than the locomotives they were replacing, the Collett 0-6-0s allocated to the
line were in such poor mechanical order that it soon became
necessary to withdraw some of them to obtain spares to keep the
others running. There was also a brief return of the Stanier
Class 3 2-6-2 tanks but again these were in such poor condition
that they were withdrawn soon after arrival on the line. The
year also saw the official withdrawal of the last of the ex-
Midland 0-4-4 tanks in the shape of No 58086 which had been
stored unserviceable at Bath for several years.

For the summer of 1961 the Class 9 2-10-0s returned in the
form of Nos 92000, 92001, 92006 and 92212, all having double
chimneys. Several of the Class 4 4-6-0s had been repaired at
Eastleigh and came back similarly fitted with double chimneys.
Standard Class 3 2-6-2 tanks were allocated to Bath and Templecombe and 0-6-0 pannier-tank No 4691 was sent to help work
the branch services.

A policy of running down the services over the Somerset &
Dorset was being followed with the traffic being diverted on to
other lines. It was thus announced that after the summer of
1962 no more through trains from the Midlands and the North
would run over the line and the Pines Express would be
diverted via Wolverhampton, Birmingham (Snow Hill) and
Oxford. Even this revised service lasted only a few years. With
the electrification of the Manchester and Liverpool lines into
Euston and of the Bournemouth line from Waterloo it was
quicker to travel via London. The usual batch of Class 9
2-10-0s was allocated to Bath for the summer and they were
joined, in August, by No 92220 *Evening Star* which was used to
haul the Pines Express on the last day. Even in this final year
of through working it was necessary to borrow locomotives, not
only Bulleid Pacifics from Bournemouth, but visitors from the

North as well. At the height of the season on 4 August no less than three Stanier Class 5s from Stoke-on-Trent were being used over the line.

Following removal of the through trains no attempt was made to rationalise the local services and they continued to run to give connections with trains that no longer existed. At the end of 1963 freight facilities were withdrawn from many stations and closed completely at the end of 1965. Many stations were reduced to unstaffed halts and the motive power reduced to a minimum. By the middle of 1963 the last of the Collett 0-6-0s were withdrawn and for the first time since the Fowlers arrived in 1874 the line was without an 0-6-0 locomotive. Late arrivals on the scene were the BR Class 4 2-6-4 tanks, which were used to work the main line trains in conjunction with the Class 4 4-6-0s. The Stanier 8F 2-8-0s had charge of the dwindling coal traffic while the Branch was completely in the hands of the Ivatt Class 2 2-6-2 tanks.

The first closure to directly affect the Somerset & Dorset was that of Bournemouth West Station on 4 October 1965. Trains were either diverted to Bournemouth Central or terminated at Branksome. Complete closure of the line was announced for September 1965 but the objections had to be heard and it was postponed until 9 January 1966. This was to be a big day for Western Region motive power and they announced that from that day all remaining services would be diesel hauled. Unfortunately for them one of the local bus operators withdrew his application for a licence and the Somerset & Dorset steam services had to stagger on until 1 March when the line was finally closed.

CHAPTER TWELVE

THE LOCOMOTIVE SUPERINTENDENTS,
1862 to 1929

The first locomotives for the Somerset Central Railway were ordered on 2 February 1861 from George England & Co of Hatcham Iron Works, London, to designs prepared by the Company's engineer, C. M. Gregory, and James Pearson of the Bristol & Exeter Railway. Since Gregory had no experience of engine management or operation he advised the directors to appoint a locomotive superintendent at an early date, but nevertheless it was August 1861 before action was taken and the services of Robert Andrews engaged at a salary of £250 per annum. His engineering career had commenced in the docks at Liverpool and later he worked in the drawing office of Beyer Peacock & Co for a time before entering the Gorton Works of the Manchester, Sheffield & Lincolnshire Railway as an Erecting Shop foreman. After the amalgamation of the Somerset Central and Dorset Central railways, he continued in office until April 1868 when the Court of Chancery, having taken control of Somerset & Dorset affairs, insisted on the stringent economy. As a result the offices of locomotive superintendent and storekeeper were abolished as separate appointments and the two departments placed under control of the Civil Engineer, F. G. Slessor. On leaving the line Andrews found employment at Nine Elms Works until March 1876 when he joined the Locomotive Department of the London, Chatham & Dover Railway.

The Receivers were discharged in May 1870 when the Court

of Chancery returned the line to the directors. Unfortunately, money remained tight and the strictest economy had still to be practised so Slessor was left in charge at Highbridge for three more years until the requirements of the Bath Extension made it essential for the appointment of a fully competent locomotive engineer. The directors asked advice from W. G. Beattie of the London & South Western Railway who suggested B. S. Fisher of the Taff Vale Railway at a salary not exceeding £300 per annum. Accepting this advice Fisher was called for interview and on being found eminently suitable for the post was appointed on 27 August 1873. The directors were particularly impressed by his thorough knowledge of engineering practice and experience of operating the goods and passenger services of a small railway with but a modicum of equipment and a largely unskilled staff. These, of course, were essential attributes of a Somerset & Dorset locomotive superintendent, and were to remain so for some years after the line was leased by the Midland and London & South Western railways.

Fisher also proved to have a natural flair for organisation and to be an excellent manager of men, it being said that he knew every employee on the line by Christian name within a month of taking office. His conversation was always enlightening and invariably contained those quick flashes of perceptive wit so endearing to all grades of railwaymen. No one ever recalled hearing him employ bad language no matter what the provocation. Behind his back he was usually referred to as 'Noggin' on account of his habit of recommending any man with a cold or chill to drink a noggin of rum after meals and a double measure on going to bed.

His presence at Highbridge was therefore quickly felt and his importance to the line increased with time. Indeed, to such a degree that after control passed to the Midland and London & South Western railways he was recommended by S. W. Johnson and W. G. Beattie as resident locomotive superintendent. This the managing committee accepted, although they raised the proposed salary by £50 to £400 per annum because of the greater responsibility of the Joint line and to forestall a possible move to a larger railway. A further rise of £50 was awarded in November 1881. Unfortunately, over the years he formed the dangerous habit of using the sidings alongside the works at Highbridge as a short cut to and from his place of residence and since he had become a little deaf the inevitable accident occurred on 10 May 1883. He was crushed between the buffers of two loaded coal wagons and was killed instantly.

Little time was lost at Derby in finding a suitable successor and on 17 May W. H. French reached the line from the Midland Railway at Leicester. The salary of £300 suggests a down grading of the appointment with greater responsibility being accepted by Johnson. French was never very happy in Somerset and when a transfer back to the parent company had been refused he resigned and retired from railway service. Later he is thought to have worked as graving dock engineer for Southampton Docks Company.

A. W. Whitaker then took charge at a salary of £375 on 1 November 1889, and it was he who instigated the supply of Derby-built 'quality' engines to the line rather than those of outside contractors as provided hitherto. He was a former pupil of Matthew Kirtley, and had been in charge of the Midland locomotive depots at Bradford, Carlisle and Leeds before his transfer to Highbridge. In all aspects of his profession he was completely and utterly Midland, and within a year of taking control had introduced the Derby system of templates and gauges together with accurate manufacturing methods to close tolerances which enabled the interchangeability of replacement parts between engines of the same class. Engines to be rebuilt or reboilered were stripped right down and a special stand provided for the initial stages of re-erection, and upon which the registration and final machining of the main frames, cylinders, slide blocks, cross stays, etc, was undertaken.

At the same time the buildings at Highbridge were modernised and extended as well as being re-equipped with second-hand machinery from Derby. All the foremen and many skilled employees were dispatched to Derby to gain experience of modern techniques and to discuss everyday problems with men

of similar responsibility. On return the newly acquired knowledge was applied so well that before many years had passed
Highbridge became known as the Crewe of the West.

Whitaker was also an inventor of some eminence and when
it was found that a large overhead travelling crane could not be
fitted without the provision of stronger foundations he designed
a locomotive traverser for the Erecting Shop. This permitted an
engine wheeled and ready for return to traffic to be quickly
transferred to an adjoining road without interference to work
being performed elsewhere in the shop. It remained in use until
Highbridge closed down. Whitaker's inventive mind was also
available to the line at large and his token-exchange apparatus
for use on the sections of single track and his water tank depth
gauge gained universal acclaim and both saw use on other railways in this country and abroad. On occasions, however,
theory and practice failed to concur and his spark arrester was
found of little value and usually resided at the rear of the running sheds.

Whitaker without doubt was the Somerset & Dorset's outstanding locomotive superintendent. It was he who introduced
4-4-0s to the line, a type that worked the express services for
over forty years, while if he had been allowed his way the goods
services would have been handled by eight-coupled engines
long before his retirement on 24 July 1911. Notwithstanding
this excellent record over no less than twenty-two years, the
managing committee refused to add to his Midland Railway
pension. However, this display of niggardliness did not stop his
coming back to the line from February 1915 to January 1919 as
acting locomotive superintendent when R. C. Archbutt was
away with the Railway Operating Division.

Yet again the replacement came from the Midland, on this
occasion from Derby itself, where M. F. Ryan for some years
had been in charge of the District Locomotive Department.
During his brief stay at Highbridge he reorganised the Boiler
Shop, persuaded Derby to provide 2-8-0s for the mineral services and instituted the practice of painting the names of
drivers in the cabs of express engines. On 13 September 1913

FOX, WALKER CONVERSIONS

Page 189 (*Top*) 0-6-0 No 1 converted in 1888 from a saddle tank engine No 1. (*Middle*) 0-6-0T No 8. 1889 conversion from 0-6-0ST No 8. (*Bottom*) 0-6-0 No 8 converted in 1908 from 0-6-0T No 8 above. Seen here with later straight-sided chimney

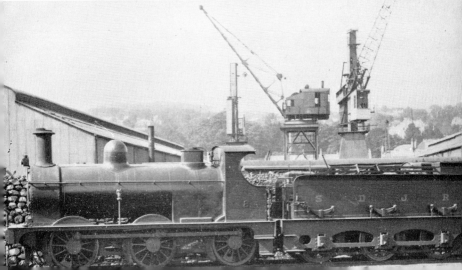

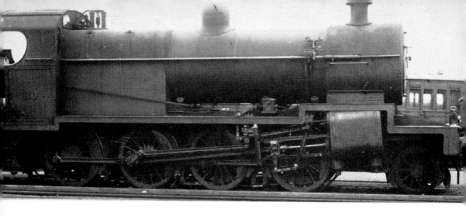

THE LATER GOODS ENGINES

Page 190   (*Top*) 2-8-0 No 80 with cut down boiler fittings. (*Middle*) 0-6-0 No 57 (one of the Armstrongs) seen here at Bath in 1929. (*Bottom*) 0-6-0TS Nos 24 and 25 at Templecombe shortly after delivery in 1929

THE RADSTOCK SHUNTERS

Page 191 (*Top*) 0-4-0ST No 45 *Bristol*, the first engine to be used in place of horses for shunting at Radstock. (*Middle*) 0-4-2ST No 25A and 0-4-0ST No 26A in Radstock engine shed. (*Bottom*) The final form of Radstock shunter. 200hp Sentinel No 101 at Radstock in 1929

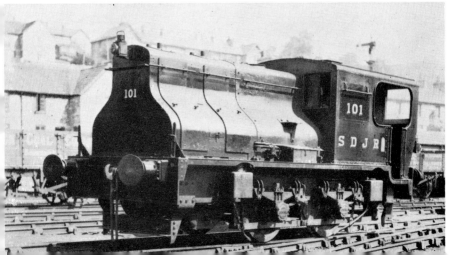

S & DJR TRAINS

Page 192 (*Top*) Small Johnson 4-4-0 No 18 at Bournemouth West waiting to depart with an up train. (*Middle*) Rebuilt Fowler 0-6-0 No 23 receives an oiling while pausing at Blandford with a down goods train. (*Bottom*) The Highbridge Works train which ran between Highbridge and Burnham to carry works employees. Seen here with 0-4-4T No 53 at Highbridge

he resigned on being promoted assistant to Robert Urie, locomotive superintendent of the London & South Western Railway, where he remained for some years before becoming
general manager of the Buenos Aires & Pacific Railway, South
America—a 5ft 3in gauge line renowned until recent years for
its massive passenger and goods 4-8-os.

The last resident locomotive superintendent was R. C.
Archbutt who took office at a salary of £250 per annum on 1
October 1913. He, too, was a Midland man and in 1930 returned to the Midland Division of the LMS. Shortly after reaching Highbridge, he prepared power classifications for both
goods and passenger engines, and following the introduction of
the 2-8-os ordered by his predecessor was able to abolish much
of the double heading which had plagued the goods services for
over a decade. Later still, following his return from the armed
forces, he replaced the 1914 power classification by an improved system based on that in use on the Midland. The
coding was painted on the cab sidesheets above the name of the
running shed to which an engine was allocated.

CHAPTER THIRTEEN

HIGHBRIDGE WORKS

On 28 August 1861 the original lease of the Somerset Central by the Bristol & Exeter Railway was due to expire and the company would have to operate its own services. Anticipating this the directors instructed the preparation of plans for standard-gauge stock and in February 1861 placed orders with a number of reputable manufacturers. Instructions were also given for the purchase of land at Highbridge and the construction thereon of buildings necessary for their maintenance and repair. By February 1862 the first buildings were occupied and by mid-April seven men and four boys were engaged modifying the buffering and coupling arrangements of the coaching stock which experience had shown to be of over-light construction. One of the tender engines suffered a pitch-in on 2 August 1862, but the works possessed no means of lifting the boiler out of the frames so resort had to be made to the Salisbury breakdown crane of the London & South Western Railway at a charge of £28.

As a result the directors authorised the purchase of more equipment and the erection of an additional building for use as a smith's shop. Even as late as October 1875 a Board of Trade inspector severely criticised the company for not having the means anywhere on the system of weighing locomotives and tenders. The important task of setting the springs and therefore the weight distribution was entrusted to the Erecting Shop foreman's judgement. A second-hand weigh-house was obtained from Nine Elms in August 1877, but for some reason was not erected at Highbridge until October 1878. Later a saw mill, larger offices, a drawing office, more storage space, a Boiler Shop and a reservoir were added, but it was not until A Whitaker became resident locomotive engineer in November 1889 that Highbridge was referred to as the Crewe of Somerset. Hitherto Derby had frequently complained of poor workmanship and of delays of up to eighteen months often suffered by engines awaiting entry to shops, but by modernising and expanding the facilities and co-ordinating the various repair stages the average time out of traffic was reduced to forty-three days while the quality of work approached that of the parent company. This improvement was materially assisted by a locomotive traverser designed and assembled by Whitaker by which engines in the Erecting Shop could be moved from one track to another using a single crane. It consisted of an inclined ramp with a trolley on which the front end of the engine was placed, then the rear end was lifted by the crane and, by releasing the trolley brake, the engine could be moved sideways, down the ramp at the front end, by the crane at the rear. Only a handful of new engines were constructed at Highbridge, but reboilerings were legion and some of the rebuilding was so extensive that many railways would have automatically accepted the resultant product as an addition to stock. In the early days complete boilers were built, although latterly resort was made to Derby.

In anticipation of having to maintain the superheated boilers of the new 4-4-0s and 2-8-0s the Boiler Shop was extended and re-equipped in 1914-15 with second-hand machinery displaced from Derby while in early 1915 the Paint Shop was modified to give better natural lighting as well as being fitted with an improved means of heating for the winter months.

A special ceremony was held at the works on 8 May 1922 when a plaque to commemorate those fallen in World War I was unveiled by the Bishop of Bath and Wells. Later the plaque was removed to the station buildings and finally to a garden of remembrance.

At the peak of its capacity over three hundred men and boys were employed in the works at Highbridge and its closure following the absorption of the locomotive stock by the LMS was a bitter blow to the town for, like Crewe and Ashford, it had grown up round the railway. Officially the closure was scheduled for 1 January 1930, but in fact there was a gradual run down over several months and work finally ceased in March that year. The last engines to receive heavy repairs were 2-8-0 No 9678 and 0-6-0 No 2883. The buildings were stripped of all useful fittings and lay derelict until World War II when they were used as a store for military equipment. After hostilities ceased attempts were made to interest local firms in the site, but the only success was to lease the Carriage & Wagon Works for several years as a piggery. A fire in the mid-1950s destroyed these buildings and the empty shell of the Locomotive Works remained for a period cluttered with the litter of gypsies who periodically wintered there. At the time of writing the majority of the works buildings have been pulled down to make room for a siding on which pulverised fly-ash was unloaded for use in the foundations of a nearby stretch of motorway.

CHAPTER FOURTEEN

THE LOCOMOTIVE LIVERIES

1861 TO 1875

Little detailed information is available concerning the liveries of the earliest engines, although from references in the press and the company's record books a reasonably accurate knowledge can be obtained. The 1861 series must have been painted dark green with black lining because when Nos 9 and 10 were accepted two years later the chairman wrote to the makers complaining that although the same dark green had been used the lining bands were red instead of the black previously used. No 11, the Great Exhibition 2-4-0 tank, had been specially painted blue with red and gold lining by the makers, George England & Co, and it was in this livery that it reached the Somerset & Dorset. To some extent this anticipated the colour adopted by Highbridge in 1886. Nos 12 to 15 apparently were delivered correctly painted since the letter of acceptance only mentioned several minor mechanical faults while the two Cudworth engines of 1865 were received in the full South Eastern Railway livery. At first the only means of identification was by brass numerals on the chimney fronts, but by 1865 tender engines had the leading and trailing splashers displaying s & DR and their numbers. No 11 had both the company's initials and its number inscribed on the side tanks. All engines had s & DR painted on the buffer beams and most retained the brass chimney numerals.

During the 1860s Highbridge employed a dark green of much the same hue as that found on the 1861 engines, but thereafter the colour was gradually darkened until by 1870-1 the lining

was omitted and after a few weeks' weathering the livery
appeared black. Later a return was made to a lighter green of a
shade much akin to that favoured in later years by Harry Wain-
wright of the South Eastern & Chatham Railway. The 1874
Fowler 0-6-0s were so painted, the black bands being bordered
by yellow lines. Combined number and ownership plates were
attached to cab sides. The first five Fox, Walker saddle tanks
were similarly painted apart from having gold-leaf numerals
instead of numberplates.

1876 TO 1884

Shortly after Derby accepted control of the line's locomotive
affairs Johnson introduced his standard Midland livery of
bluish-green relieved by black bands edged with fine white
lines. The framing was of the same colour and not the reddish-
brown favoured by many mid-Victorian locomotive superintendents. Brass numerals were attached to the cab sides of tender
or saddle tank engines and placed centrally on the tank sides of
other tank engines. Johnson visited Highbridge on 2 February
1876 and inspected 2-4-0 No 11 in the new livery, so presumably it was the first engine to receive Midland colours.

1885 TO 1886

At Derby Johnson had experimentally painted a number of
engines red towards the end of 1881, but no decision regarding
a change of livery had been taken before October 1883 when he
reported to the locomotive committee that a saving of £2,000
per annum was possible by substituting this colour for green on
both passenger and goods stock. Authorisation was then granted
for the painting of all engines red, including those working on
the Somerset & Dorset. The average cost was estimated at
£12 4s 7d (£12·23) per engine. The edging was in black with
yellow lining, while the boiler bands were also black, again
with yellow lining. As before the raised brass numerals were
attached to the cab or tank sides. Officially this magnificent
crimson lake was known as oxide-of-iron, although a less
accurate description would be difficult to imagine. Notwith-

standing the intent, no Joint engines appeared in red during 1884, all repaints as well as the new o-6-os Nos 46 to 51 being green. Probably all outstanding stocks of this colour were sent to Highbridge to be used up. As a result it was early 1885 with the delivery of the Vulcan Foundry bogie tanks Nos 52 to 55 before engines in the new colour could be seen regularly on the Somerset & Dorset. Even so Highbridge could only have painted a few older engines red because in March 1886 the well-known and much-admired blue livery was adopted. In September 1902 five six-coupled goods on order for the Midland were diverted to the Somerset & Dorset and arrived painted red while bogie tank No 1305 purchased from Derby in 1921 similarly ran for a year or so in Midland colours. Otherwise the only red liveried engines seen on Joint metals were those on trial or loan from Derby.

1886 TO 1929

No reference to the change of livery is made in the company's record books, but William Adams was sent by the LSWR locomotive committee in April 1886 to investigate the wearing properties of the Midland red and Somerset & Dorset blue liveries. In the following month he reported that the South Western's green was cheaper to apply and equally long wearing and suggested that it should be employed by Highbridge Works instead of the Prussian blue recently introduced. Fortunately, the Joint committee disagreed as the latter was one of the most attractive of the pre-grouping liveries and one employed until its locomotives passed to LMS control. The lining was in black with a fine yellow line on either side while the buffer beams were vermilion, with black edging, again divided by a yellow line. The cut-out brass numerals remained on the cab sides or centralised on the side tanks, in the case of the passenger tanks having the company's coat of arms above and on the passenger tender engines on the leading splashers. No coat of arms was provided for the Fox, Walker saddle tanks or the goods classes, although like the passenger engines their buffer beams had SDJR inscribed in gold leaf. Usually both front and rear buffer beams were so lettered, but some goods engines had the latter left blank while for many years the Fox, Walkers had rectangular numberplates attached to the bunker back plates.

About 1894 the tender and tank sides were lettered SDJR in gold leaf. For a time the passenger tanks retained the brass numerals on their side tanks, these being flanked on each side by two of the initials and topped by the coat of arms, then the numerals were resited on the bunker sides and the coat of arms centralised between the lettering. The passenger tender classes retained the cabside numerals and the leading splasher coat of arms while the goods tender classes also remained as before apart from the tender lettering. Goods tanks with short bunkers had their numerals on the cab sidesheets where more space was available.

This remained the standard livery until 1914 when the 2-8-0s delivered by Derby appeared in unlined black with Midland-style smokebox door numberplates. Fortunately, this depressing livery was not applied to 4-4-0s Nos 70 and 71 built at the same time and they arrived resplendent in blue together with smokebox door numberplates. Over the next few years the goods tanks gradually succumbed to the unlined black while in August 1921 this was standardised for the six-coupled goods as well.

Other changes around this period for new stock included transfer numerals in place of the cut-out brass numbers and plain buffer beams. Older engines, however, usually retained SDJR lettered buffer beams, but some had this abbreviated to SD. Additions were the power classifications high up the cab sidesheeting and the allocation in small lettering above the handrailing.

Blue appeared again on goods engines in early 1929 when the seven standard LMS six-coupled tanks were delivered by W. G. Bagnall Ltd, but at the same time the directors were considering the use of a cheaper livery and in May 1929 had 4-4-0 No 18 experimentally painted black with red lining. The coat of arms remained on the leading splashers, but the buffer beams were plain red and transfer figures replaced the brass numerals on the cab sides while a numberplate appeared on the smokebox door. Probably because of the necessity to utilise the available supplies of blue paint no other engines were similarly treated before the LMS take-over. Then the black livery of that company was used for both goods and passenger engines.

CHAPTER FIFTEEN

LOCOMOTIVE CLASSIFICATION

The first mention of a locomotive classification occurred on 15 January 1889 when five C Class boilers were ordered from Derby for use on the Johnson bogie tanks. Apparently it was only intended to differentiate between the various types of locomotive then in service because it consisted simply of a lettered code. New construction was added to the list until 0-6-0s Nos 72 to 76 entered traffic towards the end of 1902 when all further additions to stock were given their equivalent Midland terminology. The class letters were still used in correspondence between Highbridge and Derby for some years,

Letter		*Engine types & Nos*	
A	Johnson	4-4-0s	Nos 14 to 18, 45, 67, 68
B	Old 2-4-0s		Nos 15A to 18A
C	Johnson	0-4-4T	Nos 10 to 13, 14A, 29 to 32, 52 to 55
D	England	2-4-0T	No 27A
E	England	2-4-0ST	No 28A
F	Fox, Walker	0-6-0	No 1
G	Johnson 4ft 6in	0-6-0s	Nos 25 to 28, 33 to 44, 46 to 51, 56 to 61
	Fowler	0-6-0s	Nos 19 to 24
H	Johnson 5ft 2in	0-6-0s	Nos 62 to 66, 72 to 76
J	Fox, Walker	0-6-0T	No 8
K	Fox, Walker	0-6-0ST	Nos 2 to 7, 9
L	Highbridge	0-4-2ST	No 25A
M	Highbridge	0-4-0ST	Nos 26A, 45A

although as time passed the small 0-6-0s were generally referred to as the Fowler and Scottie classes while the Johnson passenger tanks became the s & d bogie tank engines. Details of this list are shown on the previous page.

The next scheme was introduced by R. C. Archbutt who took office as resident locomotive superintendent on 13 September 1913. It was based on loading, the passenger locomotives being divided into three groups and the goods into four. The smaller engines were not listed for obvious reasons. The following list was published on 31 December 1917, but only the passenger classes were actually quoted by tonnage.

Passenger classes:

Group I	0-4-4T	Nos 10 to 13, 14A, 29 to 32, 52 to 55	140 tons
Group II	4-4-0	Nos 14 to 18, 45, 67 to 69, 77, 78	170 tons
Group III	4-4-0	Nos 70, 71	215 tons

Goods classes:

Group I	0-6-0	Nos 8, 25 to 28, 33 to 44, 56 to 61
Group II	0-6-0	Nos 19 to 24, 56 to 62, 64, 65, 72 to 76
Group III	0-6-0ST	Nos 1 to 7, 9
	0-6-0	Nos 63, 66
Group IV	2-8-0	Nos 80 to 85

This system of classification had obvious limitations and in 1923 was replaced by an entirely new scheme which was based on that employed by the Midland Railway. It differed, however, by using 'p' and 'g' ratings whereas the current Midland–lms power classification consisted of numbers alone. The higher the number, then the greater the power potentiality. Apparently the lms found its system too limiting since in 1928 a change was made to the Somerset & Dorset concept, although the symbols of 'p' and 'f' were used for passenger and goods ratings.

The exact date that the third and final Somerset & Dorset classification came into operation is not known but it must have been about May 1923 since a photograph of the Johnson 5ft 2in 0-6-0 No 62 at Highbridge shows the power rating 4P 3G painted high up on the cab sidesheets. At the time this engine was recently ex-works. The scheme was not without teething troubles for experience showed that some classes could be safely upgraded while others required relegation. Details are as follows:

Original classification		Revised classification		Class
	2G		—	Fox, Walker saddle tanks
1P	1G		—	Johnson Scottie 0-6-0s, 0-4-4 tanks and 0-6-0 No 8
1P	2G		—	Fowler 0-6-0s
2P	1G	2P	2G	Small Johnson 4-4-0s (reboiled)
3P	2G	2P	2G	4-4-0s Nos 77, 78
3P	3G		—	LMS 0-6-0T
4P	2G	3P	2G	Superheated 4-4-0s (a)
4P	3G	3P	3G	Johnson 5ft 3in 0-6-0 (large boilered rebuilds)
5P	4G	4P	4G	Fowler Class 4 0-6-0s
5P	5G		—	Both series of 2-8-0s

(a) Nos 44 to 46 were delivered as 2P, but this was immediately changed to 3P 2G.

When the LMS took the Somerset & Dorset locomotives into stock then that company's classification was substituted, details being as follows:

1P	All 0-4-4 tanks	3F	Johnson 5ft 2in 0-6-0s, LMS 0-6-0 tanks
2P	All 4-4-0s		
1F	Johnson 4ft 6in 0-6-0s	4F	Fowler Class 4 0-6-0s
2F	Fox, Walker saddle tanks	7F	2-8-0s

LMS RENUMBERING OF SOMERSET & DORSET LOCOMOTIVES

S & D 1929 No	LMS 1930 No	Type	LMS Power Class	S & D 1929 No	LMS 1930 No	Type	LMS Power Class
			2F	22	7153	,,	,,
			,,	23	7154	,,	,,
			,,	24	7155	,,	,,
			,,	25	7156	,,	,,
			,,	29A	1205	0-4-4T	1P
			,,	30A	1206	,,	,,
			,,	31A	1207	,,	,,
			,,	34	2880	0-6-0	1F
			1P	35	2881	,,	,,
			,,	36	2882	,,	,,
			,,	37	2883	,,	,,
			,,	38	2884	,,	,,
			,,	39	322	4-4-0	2P
14	(300)	,,	2P	40	323	,,	,,
15	301	,,	,,	41	324	,,	,,
17	302	,,	,,	42	325	,,	,,
18	303	,,	,,	43	326	,,	,,
19	7150	0-6-0T	3F	44	633	4-4-0	2P
20	7151	,,	,,	45	634	,,	,,
21	7152	,,	,,	46	635	,,	,,
51	2885	0-6-0	1F	72	3216	0-6-0	3F
52	1230	0-4-4T	1P	73	3218	,,	,,
53	1231	,,	,,	74	3228	,,	,,
54	1305	,,	,,	75	3248	,,	,,
55	1232	,,	,,	76	3260	,,	,,
57	4557	0-6-0	4F	77	320	4-4-0	2P
58	4558	,,	,,	78	321	,,	,,
59	4559	,,	,,	80	9670	2-8-0	7F
60	4560	,,	,,	81	9671	,,	,,
61	4561	,,	,,	82	9672	,,	,,
62	3194	0-6-0	3F	83	9673	,,	,,
63	3198	,,	,,	84	9674	,,	,,
64	3201	,,	,,	85	9675	,,	,,
65	3204	,,	,,	86	9676	,,	,,
66	3211	,,	,,	87	9677	,,	,,
67	2886	0-6-0	1F	88	9678	,,	,,
68	2887	,,	,,	89	9679	,,	,,
69	2888	,,	,,	90	9680	,,	,,
70	2889	,,	,,	101	7190	SENTINEL	—
71	2890	,,	,,	102	7191	,,	—

APPENDIX: SOMERSET & DORSET LOCOMOTIVES

THE EARLY LOCOMOTIVES

Engine No	Maker	Date	Reboilered	Remarks	Withdrawn
1	G. England	10/1861	—	Sold Fox, Walker & Co	11/1874
2	,,	11/1861	—	To No 25 6/1876; 25A 8/1881	5/1885
3	,,	,,	—	Sold Fox, Walker & Co	11/1874
4	,,	,,	—	,,	,,
5	,,	,,	—	,,	1/1875
6	,,	,,	—	To No 26 6/1876; 26A 8/1881. Rebuilt 2-4-0T 5/1884	1/1889
7	,,	,,	5/1888, 7/1902	To No 27 6/1876; 27A 8/1881. Rebuilt 2-4-0T 5/1888	7/1925
8	,,	,,	1/1883, 10/1904	To No 28 7/1876; 28A 8/1881. Rebuilt 2-4-0ST 1/1883; 2-4-0T 10/1904	4/1928
17	,,	11/1865	8/1879	To 17A 5/1891; 45 11/1895	1/1897
18	,,	,,	3/1879	To 18A 5/1891	1/1897
19	Vulcan Foundry (562)	7/1866	12/1880	To No 15 2/1871; 15A 5/1891	1/1914
20	,, (563)	,,	6/1881	To No 16 2/1871; 16A 5/1891	1/1914
19	J. Fowler & Co (2125)	3/1874	5/1888, 3/1908	—	6/1927
20	,, (2126)	4/1874	2/1893, 12/1910	—	8/1928
21	,, (2127)	5/1874	9/1893, 2/1911	—	7/1928
22	,, (2128)	6/1874	11/1892, 11/1911	—	8/1928
23	,, (2129)	7/1874	8/1892, 6/1910	—	8/1928
24	,, (2130)	8/1874	11/1893, 10/1910	—	8/1928

THE EARLY LOCOMOTIVES—(continued)

Engine No	Maker		Date	Reboilered	LMS No	Withdrawn
1	Fox, Walker & Co	(254)	7/1874	1/1888 (0-6-0); 12/1908 (0-6-0ST)	1500	11/1930
2	,,	(255)	8/1874	8/1885 & 9/1906	(1501)	2/1930
3	,,	(256)	9/1874	4/1893 & 7/1911	1502	9/1930
4	,,	(257)	2/1875	10/1890 & 4/1909	(1503)	2/1930
5	,,	(258)	2/1875	3/1890 & 2/1910	1504	11/1934
6	,,	(320)	6/1876	12/1894 & 4/1911	1505	11/1934
7	,,	(321)	6/1876	5/1890 & 10/1909	1506	10/1934
8	,,	(322)	8/1876	11/1889 (0-6-0T); 10/1908 (0-6-0)	—	5/1928
9	,,	(323)	8/1876	7/1899 & 4/1910	1507	12/1930

THE JOHNSON BOGIE TANKS

Engine No	Maker		Date	Re-boilered	Renumbered	LMS No	Withdrawn
10	Avonside Engine Co	(1184)	11/1877	1/1891, 3/1907	—	(1200)	2/1930
11	,,	(1185)	,,	2/1892, 10/1909	—	1201	9/1930
12	,,	(1187)	,,	3/1890, 1/1907	—	1202	10/1931
13	,,	(1188)	12/1877	10/1894, 10/1906	—	1203	11/1930
14	,,	(1189)	,,	7/1891, 12/1907	14A 2/1897	(1204)	4/1930
29	,,	(1186)	11/1877	11/1889, 4/1907	29A 4/1926	1205	12/1930
30	,,	(1190)	12/1877	8/1893, 9/1906	30A 4/1926	1206	5/1932
31	,,	(1191)	,,	4/1891, 10/1910	31A 4/1926	1207	12/1932
32	,,	(1192)	,,	12/1893, 2/1907, 3/1925	52 8/1928	1230	6/1946
52	Vulcan Foundry	(1071)	12/1884	9/1902	—	—	5/1928
53	,,	(1072)	1/1885	3/1905, 1/1926	—	1231	3/1930
54	,,	(1073)	,,	6/1907	—	—	11/1920
55	,,	(1074)	,,	8/1906, 6/1925	—	1232	12/1932
54	Midland Rly		4/1884	3/1902, 7/1918	ex-MR 1305 & 1651	1305	8/1931

THE SMALL 4-4-0S

Engine No	Maker	Date	Reboilered	LMS No	Withdrawn
15	Derby Works	5/1891	4/1905, 9/1910	—	8/1928
16	,,	,,	4/1906, 4/1910	—	8/1928
17	,,	,,	8/1904, 1/1908, 11/1927	302	6/1931
18	,,	,,	12/1904, 6/1911. To No 15 8/1928	301	9/1931
67	,,	1/1896	12/1907	—	8/1920
68	,,	,,	5/1908	—	11/1921
14	,,	2/1897	12/1910	(300)	1/1930
45	,,	,,	8/1909, 9/1926. To No 18 8/1928	303	2/1932

THE LARGE 4-4-0S

Engine No	Maker	Date	Reboilered	LMS No	Withdrawn
69	Derby Works	11/1903	—	—	4/1921
70	,,	,,	—	—	4/1914
71	,,	,,	—	—	5/1914
77	,,	3/1908	5/1926	320	9/1931
78	,,	,,	11/1921	321	3/1938
70 (later No 39)	,,	5/1914	—	322	3/1953
71 (,, No 40)	,,	4/1914	—	323	9/1956
67 (,, No 41)	,,	4/1921	—	324	1/1953
68 (,, No 42)	,,	4/1921	—	325	10/1951
69 (,, No 43)	,,	4/1921	—	326	5/1956
44	,,	6/1928	—	633	11/1959
45	,,	6/1928	—	634	5/1962
46	,,	7/1928	—	635	2/1961

THE SCOTTIE GOODS

Engine No	Maker	Date	Reboilered			LMS No	Withdrawn
			Johnson	Deeley–Johnson	G5		
33	Neilson & Co (2269)	6/1878	12/1890	—			10/1914
34	„ (2270)	7/1878	3/1891	—			10/1914
35	„ (2271)	„	5/1889, 6/1903	—			4/1922
36	„ (2272)	„	10/1889, 11/1898	—			„
37	„ (2273)	„	4/1893, 6/1903, 1/1914	—			„
38	„ (2274)	„	3/1897	—			„
39	Vulcan Foundry (840)	12/1879	1/1896	—			4/1925
40	(67 8/1928) „ (841)	„	1/1890, 4/1898	9/1908		2886	12/1930
41	„ (842)	„	2/1896	—			7/1925
42	(68 8/1928) „ (843)	1/1880	6/1890, 10/1898	—		2887	11/1932
43	„ (844)	„	7/1891, 10/1901	—			10/1914
44	(69 8/1928) „ (845)	„	8/1890, 1/1914	12/1908, 5/1929		2888	12/1930
25	Vulcan Foundry (896)	7/1881	9/1903	—			12/1928
26	„ (897)	8/1881	1/1897	11/1908			12/1928
27	„ (898)	„	5/1892, 7/1899	—			10/1914
28	„ (899)	„	11/1891, 1/1900	7/1908			12/1928
46	„ (1055)	8/1884	2/1903	—			9/1925
47	(70 8/1928) „ (1056)	„	11/1900	—		2889	11/1932
48	„ (1057)	„	5/1903	—			4/1925
49	(71 8/1928) „ (1058)	„	11/1903	11/1928		2890	10/1932
50	(51 8/1928) „ (1059)	9/1884	4/1901	—		2885	2/1931
51	„ (1060)	10/1884	1/1903	—			11/1925
56	(33 4/1922) „ (1264)	6/1890	—	10/1906			10/1928
57	(34 „) „ (1265)	„	—	11/1906	12/1928	2880	12/1932
58	(35 4/1922) „ (1266)	„	—	1/1909	3/1929	2881	„
59	(36 „) „ (1267)	„	—	7/1907	5/1928	2882	„
60	(37 „) „ (1268)	7/1890	—	5/1908	11/1927	2883	„
61	(38 „) „ (1269)	„	—	9/1908	3/1928	2884	„

THE BULLDOGS

| Engine No | Maker | Date | Reboilered | | LMS No | BR No | With-drawn |
			H	G7			
62	Derby Works	1/1896	—	5/1923	3194	43194	12/1960
63	,,	,,	10/1914	9/1920	3198		12/1947
64	,,	2/1896	—	3/1921	3201	43201	4/1957
65	,,	,,	—	12/1921	3204	43204	9/1956
66	,,	3/1896	4/1914	5/1920	3211	43211	6/1961
72	Neilson, Reid & Co (6030)	9/1902	—	10/1925	3216	43216	8/1962
73	,, (6031)	,,	—	7/1924	3218	43218	4/1960
74	,, (6032)	,,	—	4/1924	3228	43228	10/1952
75	,, (6033)	,,	—	11/1924	3248	43248	8/1959
76	,, (6034)	,,	—	11/1923	3260	(43260)	9/1949

THE RADSTOCK SHUNTERS

Engine No	Maker	Date	Pur-chased	Re-boilered	With-drawn
45 (45A)	Slaughter, Gruning & Co	1852	10/1882	4/1883	11/1895
Bristol					
25A	Highbridge Works	12/1885	—	10/1896	2/1929
26A	,,	10/1895	—	—	12/1930
45A	,,	4/1895	—	—	8/1929
101 (LMS 7190)	Sentinel Waggon Works Ltd (7587)	2/1929	—	—	3/1961
102 (LMS 7191)	,, (7588)	5/1929	—	—	8/1959

THE 2-8-0s

Engine No	Maker		Date	Re-boilered (G9AS)	1930 LMS No	1932 LMS No	BR No	With-drawn
80	Derby Works		2/1914	—	9670	13800	53800	7/1959
81	,,		3/1914	—	9671	13801	53801	7/1961
82	,,		3/1914	—	9672	13802	53802	3/1960
83	,,		4/1914	—	9673	13803	53803	2/1962
84	,,		4/1914	—	9674	13804	53804	2/1962
85	,,		8/1914	—	9675	13805	53805	3/1961
86	Stephenson	(3892)	7/1925	8/1955	9676	13806	53806	1/1964
87	,,	(3893)	7/1925	6/1954	9677	13807	53807	10/1964
88	,,	(3894)	7/1925	12/1953	9678	13808	53808	3/1964
89	,,	(3895)	7/1925	2/1930	9679	13809	53809	6/1964
90	,,	(3896)	8/1925	2/1930	9680	13810	53810	12/1963

THE ARMSTRONGS

Engine No	Maker		Date	1930 LMS No	BR No	With-drawn
57	Armstrong, Whitworth & Co	(468)	4/1922	4557	44557	9/1962
58	,,	(469)	,,	4558	44558	12/1964
59	,,	(470)	,,	4559	44559	1/1963
60	,,	(471)	,,	4560	44560	8/1965
61	,,	(472)	,,	4561	44561	4/1962

THE JINTIES

Engine No	Maker		Date	1930 LMS No	1932 LMS No	BR No	With-drawn
19	W. G. Bagnall Ltd	(2358)	22/1928	7150	7310	47310	4/1962
20	,,	(2359)	1/1929	7151	7311	47311	12/1960
21	,,	(2360)	,,	7152	7312	47312	3/1961
22	,,	(2361)	,,	7153	7313	47313	6/1967
23	,,	(2362)	,,	7154	7314	47314	11/1966
24	,,	(2363)	2/1929	7155	7315	47315	8/1959
25	,,	(2364)	,,	7156	7316	47316	11/1962

DIMENSIONS

In a book of this nature readers expect to be given the leading dimensions of the engines concerned, but a few words of warning are necessary. The first is against the assumption that the relative powers of engines can be assessed to any degree of accuracy by comparing published dimensions. The second is that not even officially recognised figures are completely reliable for every, or even any, engine of a class. For instance, the cylinder diameter varies in all engines as the effects of wear are combated by reboring while to the same purpose wheel diameters are reduced by re-turning. Engine weights are equally inaccurate because the mystic words 'in working order' can conceal a multitude of half truths. Even under ideal circumstances (and how often were they in the days of steam?) axle-loads were extremely difficult to measure accurately while the weight of all engines tends to increase with age because of frame patching and the addition of more modern equipment.

In this history use where possible has been made of the dimensions given by the Midland Railway in their Locomotive Diagrams, although for one period Derby enhanced the heating surfaces of its boilers by taking into account in their calculations the entire length of the tubes and not as normally practised only between the tube plates. For the earlier years reliance has been placed on the dimensions quoted by the makers and the Board of Trade Accident Reports.

BIBLIOGRAPHY

BRITISH TRANSPORT HISTORICAL RECORDS (including minute books of the Somerset Central, Dorset Central, Somerset & Dorset, Midland, London & South Western and Somerset & Dorset Joint railways, locomotive registers and diagram books, drawings and miscellaneous records of the various companies involved)

JOURNALS
The Journal of the Stephenson Locomotive Society
The Railway Gazette
The Railway Observer
The Railway Magazine
The Railway World
The Locomotive and Carriage and Wagon Review
The Journal of the Institution of Locomotive Engineers
The Railway & Travel Monthly

MISCELLANEOUS
Locomotive and Train Working in the Latter Part of the Nineteenth Century, Volume 5 (E. L. AHRONS)
The Somerset & Dorset Railway (ROBIN ATTHILL)
The Somerset & Dorset Railway (BARRIE & CLINKER)
The Development of British Locomotive Design (E. L. AHRONS)
Bradshaw's Guide
Somerset & Dorset Joint Railway public and working time-tables

ACKNOWLEDGEMENTS

Thanks are due to David Tee for reading through the manuscript and making many suggestions which the authors were most pleased to accept. Thanks are also due to Brian Radford, Robin Atthill, G. A. Yeomans and W. Vaughan-Jenkins.

ILLUSTRATIONS

The sources of the illustrations are as follows:

AUTHOR'S COLLECTION: 67 (*top, middle*), 102 (*top*), 135 (*top*) 153 (*top*), 154 (*top*), 189 (*top*), 190 (*middle*), 192 (*top, middle*)

BR OFFICIAL: 67 (*bottom*), 136 (*middle*), 154 (*bottom*), 156 (*bottom*), 189 (*middle*), 191 (*top*)

H. C. CASSERLEY: 135 (*bottom*), 136 (*bottom*), 155 (*bottom*), 190 (*bottom*), 191 (*bottom*)

W. H. C. KELLAND: 33 (*top, bottom*)

B. RADFORD COLLECTION: 34 (*top, bottom*), 68 (*top, middle, bottom*), 101 (*top, bottom*), 136 (*top*), 155 (*top*), 156 (*top*), 192 (*bottom*)

REAL PHOTOS LTD: 102 (*bottom*), 189 (*bottom*), 190 (*top*), 191 (*middle*)

INDEX